The Palestinian-Israeli Accord

Look for these and other books in the Lucent Overview Series:

The Palestinian-Israeli Accord

by Phyllis Corzine

WORLD IN CONFLICT

Library of Congress Cataloging-in-Publication Data

Corzine, Phyllis, 1943–
    The Palestinian-Israeli accord / by Phyllis Corzine.
        p.   cm. — (Lucent overview series)
    Includes bibliographical references and index.
    Summary: Presents an historical overview of the events leading
up to the 1994 peace treaty between the state of Israel and the PLO.
    ISBN 1-56006-181-2 (alk. paper)
    1. Jewish-Arab relations—Juvenile literature.   2. Israel. Treaties,
etc.   Munazzamat al-Tahrīr al-Filastīnīyah, 1994 April 29—
Juvenile literature.   [1. Jewish-Arab relations.   2. Israel—
Foreign relations—Treaties.]   I. Title.   II. Series.
DS119.7.C668   1997
956.94—dc20   96–34886
                                                            CIP
                                                             AC

Copyright © 1997 by Lucent Books, Inc.
P.O. Box 289011, San Diego, CA 92198-9011
Printed in the U.S.A.

Contents

Introduction

At THE EASTERN end of the Mediterranean Sea lies a small piece of land once known as Palestine, about 280 miles long by 80 miles wide at its widest point. The land has no significant natural resources. Its fertile areas are covered in fields of grain, orange groves, and orchards, but other regions are dry, hot, and nearly barren of life. The land has no precise boundaries, and it is not a state. Today the region comprises the State of Israel, the West Bank and the Gaza Strip (both controlled by Israel), and part of the kingdom of Jordan. Though small in size, the region has been the center of conflict for thousands of years. It is a natural passageway between Egypt, to the southwest, and Syria, to the northeast, and from the Mediterranean Sea to the lands east of the Jordan River. Invaders have crisscrossed this narrow strip of land many times over the centuries, spilling the blood of many peoples. To this day, blood is spilled in the region in the fighting between Jewish and Arab inhabitants, who both believe they have a legitimate claim to the land.

Ancient claims

Jews believe their right to the land comes from God. According to the Bible, the ancient Jews were led out of Egypt to this so-called Promised Land (an event historians believe took place about 1300 B.C.). Jewish kingdoms flourished in the region for about seven hundred years, until they were conquered by neighboring kingdoms. Eventually, Rome conquered the region and called it Palestine. In A.D. 70 Romans destroyed Jerusalem's Temple, built by

King Solomon to house the Ark of the Covenant, and following a Jewish revolt in 132 they drove all Jews from their capital city of Jerusalem. Some Jews remained in northern Palestine, but most scattered to other lands and eventually migrated to countries around the world, an event known as the Diaspora. However, the idea of a return to the Promised Land has persisted in Jewish faith, symbolizing for many Jews the spiritual act of returning to God's love after being separated from him by sin. For some, a return to the Promised Land means reclaiming the land that God gave them.

During the following centuries, Palestine was occupied by other peoples, many of whom were Arabs who settled both in the cities and on farmland. Throughout the centuries, however, Jews around the world still considered the city of Jerusalem their holy city. By the twentieth century, many of the Arabs had lived on the land for generations, and they too felt that they had a claim to the region.

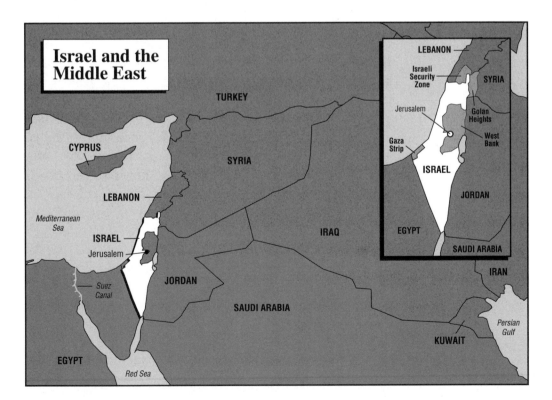

Events were further complicated when Britain and France became involved in the area and tried to negotiate conflicts between the Arabs and Jews. This foreign involvement created further resentment between the two groups. Bitterness grew between the Jews and Arabs. In 1948, the modern State of Israel was established and Jews reclaimed their ancient right to the land. Arabs of the region, who hoped to establish an independent state of Palestine that included the land claimed by the Jews, were unwilling to compromise and share the land with the Israelis. The Arabs in what had been Palestine and in surrounding Arab countries vowed to push the Israelis into the sea, and they launched an all-out war against Israel.

The Arab attempt to destroy Israel failed, but the conflict continued. Non-Jews who occupied the region eventually came to call themselves Palestinians, after the ancient land of Palestine. While many Palestinians desired peace with Israel, others organized terrorist groups of guerrilla fighters to attack and kill Israeli citizens. They still hoped to destroy Israel and establish a Palestinian state. Israel, on the other hand, retaliated for these terrorist attacks by bombing Palestinian holdouts, sometimes killing citizens who had nothing to do with the terrorism.

The violence continued for decades, often breaking out in open warfare between Israel and other Arab states who supported the Palestinian claims. The hostility threatened the stability of the entire Middle East, causing fears of a widespread war that could disrupt the flow of oil from oil-producing Arab states and that could force the United States and other nations to become involved.

A historic handshake

Since Israel's birth, the United States has steadfastly supported its ally, Israel, while trying to broker peace between Israel and the Palestinians as well as bring safety and security to Israel and the rest of the Middle East. Finally, on September 13, 1993, halfway around the world from this ancient land, a historic event took place in Washington, D.C. As people around the world watched, a hand-

shake was exchanged between two old enemies—Yasir Arafat, leader of the Palestine Liberation Organization (PLO) and Yitzhak Rabin, prime minister of Israel. The handshake sealed an agreement between the two men to bring peace between Israel and the Palestinians and to stop the bloodshed in the region once and for all. Though the signing of the accord between Israelis and Palestinians did not stop the violence, the twenty-first century still holds the promise of peace at last.

President Clinton looks on as Israeli prime minister Yitzhak Rabin (left) and Palestinian Liberation Organization leader Yasir Arafat (right) shake hands after signing the September 13, 1993, peace accord.

1

Roots of the Conflict

AT THE TURN of the century, most of the Arab Middle East was under the rule of the Ottoman Empire, which was nearing collapse. Compared to western European nations, the Ottoman Empire was backward and undeveloped, and lacked modern industry. The European states of Great Britain, Germany, France, and Russia looked greedily at the fading empire. All these nations had important

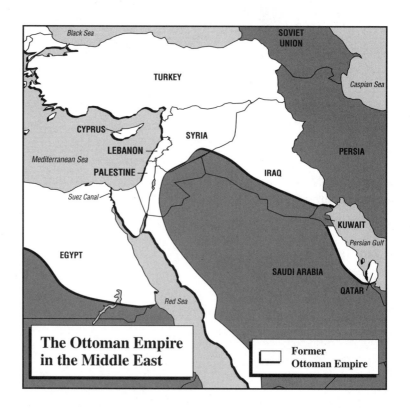

The Ottoman Empire in the Middle East

☐ Former Ottoman Empire

trading interests in the Middle East and Far East, and they hoped to expand their military and economic power by taking control of the Ottoman Empire. Great Britain was especially interested in the Middle East because it was so near Britain's most prized possession, India. Both France and Britain had already gained control of regions around the Suez Canal, an important shipping passage that halved the time required to transport goods to Europe from the Far East. These two nations would play an important role in the conflict that was brewing between Arabs and Jews.

Theodor Herzl founded the Zionist movement in the late 1800s. Zionists hoped to establish an independent Jewish state in Palestine.

Zionism

For centuries, the Jewish people had a religious and cultural identity but no formalized nation. Throughout the centuries, they had been subject to persecution and to anti-Semitism (discrimination based on their identity as Jews), especially in Europe. They had been kept on the margins of society, refused the right to practice many trades and professions. They had been the target of pogroms (organized massacres and persecutions) in which tens of thousands had been murdered. They had been driven from their homes and their property had been confiscated.

In response to these circumstances, a Hungarian newspaperman named Theodor Herzl founded a movement called Zionism in the late 1800s. Herzl was convinced that the only way for Jews to be safe from anti-Semitism was to live in a Jewish state. He and his followers believed the Jewish state should be located in the ancient Promised Land of Palestine. Zionist leaders adopted this position in the platform of their 1897 congress: "The aim of Zionism is to create for the Jewish people a home in Palestine secured by public law."

A small minority of Jews had been living in Palestine for centuries, but now European Jews began immigrating to the area. They bought land and established farms and settlements. Following World War I, this immigration increased, causing serious conflicts.

The majority of people inhabiting Palestine were Arabs who resented the influx of Jewish settlers. In 1918, Arabs in Palestine numbered about seven hundred thousand. Only fifty-six thousand were Jews. Arabs were concerned that the influx of Jews would derail their own plans for an independent Arab state. The Arabs had been under Ottoman rule for centuries, and like the Jews, wanted a state under their own political control. Both the Arabs and the Jews hoped to make Palestine the site of their independent states. Palestine would soon become a battleground of these conflicting interests as the world powers moved toward war.

World War I

When World War I broke out, Great Britain exploited the enmity between the Arabs and the Ottoman Turks by enlisting the Arabs as allies in its fight against the Ottoman Turks. In 1915, in return for an Arab rebellion against the Turks, Britain agreed to support an independent Arab state that would encompass the land from the Persian Gulf westward to the Mediterranean. In a letter to Sharif Hussein, the Arab ruler of the holy city of Mecca, British official Sir Henry McMahon wrote: "Great Britain is prepared to recognize and support the independence of the Arabs in all regions within the limits demanded by the Sharif of Mecca."

McMahon's promise later became a source of controversy, with the British claiming that they did not intend the region of Palestine to be included in their promise. The confusion over what land was promised to the Arabs was further complicated by a document called the Balfour Declaration. In 1917 another British official, Foreign Secretary Arthur Balfour, promised Britain's Lord Rothschild, member of the Zionist Federation, that

> His Majesty's Government view with favour the establishment in Palestine of a national home for the Jewish people, and will use their best endeavours to facilitate the achievement of this

object, it being clearly understood that nothing shall be done which may prejudice the civil and religious rights of the existing non-Jewish communities in Palestine, or the rights and political status enjoyed by Jews in any other country.

Thus, the British seemed to be making two mutually exclusive promises. The British desire to support a Jewish homeland may have been motivated by anti-Semitism in Britain. Jewish refugees were migrating to England to escape increasing persecution in eastern Europe. By the end of the nineteenth century, Londoners were rioting and demonstrating against the Jewish refugees. Whatever Britain's motives, the Balfour Declaration became a source of hope for Zionists throughout the world and a source of anger and frustration for Arabs in Palestine and other areas of the Middle East.

The Arabs insisted that Palestine was part of the land promised to them. When they complained to the British, they were told that Jewish settlement in Palestine would be allowed only "insofar as would be consistent with the . . . freedom of the Arab population." The British seemed

European Jews heeded the Zionist philosophy and immigrated to Palestine in the early 1900s. These pioneers established Jewish settlements and farms, which opened the floodgates for other Jews eager to find refuge in Palestine.

to be assuring the Arabs that the British would honor their commitment to independent Arab states.

The British Rule

At the end of the war in 1918, the League of Nations granted Great Britain the right to rule Palestine and Iraq, and France the right to rule Syria and Lebanon. The British divided Palestine into two parts: The area east of the Jordan River was called Transjordan (now Jordan), where the British installed an Arab ruler. The balance of Palestine was retained under British rule, with the intention of creating a Jewish homeland. To Arab nationalists—those seeking an independent Arab nation—this League of Nations arrangement simply exchanged one foreign ruler (the Ottomans) for another (the British and French). Arab nationalists wanted to bring all Arab regions under Arab rule, including Palestine, where Zionist settlers were seen as one more foreign influence that ruled Arab lands.

Thus two opposing forces were sharply divided—Arabs who wanted an independent Arab state that included Palestine and who were by far the largest percentage of the population in Palestine, and Jews who had been promised an independent Jewish state in the area of Palestine. Although it was the intent of the foreign powers, Britain and France, to create several independent Arab states plus one independent Jewish state, the Arabs believed that they were entitled to all of the land. Further, they believed that the region of Palestine had been promised to them as part of their agreement to fight against the Turks.

Tensions grow

Throughout the 1920s and 1930s, Jews continued to settle in Palestine in greater numbers. Jewish settlers bought farmland from absentee Arab owners and set up independent farming settlements called kibbutzim, often displacing Arab farmers who rented the land from its previous Arab owners. This new wave of immigrants was more militant than earlier Jewish settlers. Many believed they

should use force against the Arabs if necessary to establish a Jewish majority in Palestine. When in 1921 riots between Jews and Arabs killed 120 Arabs and 200 Jews, the Zionists organized a militia, the Haganah (Hebrew for "defense"). As the number of Jewish settlers and their landholdings increased, Arabs grew increasingly angry and frustrated. By 1929 more than 150,000 Jews lived in Palestine. That year the Jewish National Fund bought land in Palestine, evicting about 2,500 Arab farmers. The resulting Arab riots in Jerusalem and Hebron were put down by the British, but the British refused to halt Jewish immigration and land acquisition. The British did allow Iraq to gain its independence in 1932, but tensions in the region continued to grow.

In 1936 a full-scale Arab rebellion broke out. Armed bands of Arabs from Palestine, joined by Arab volunteers from Syria and Iraq, attacked both the British and the Jews. Finally, a British Royal Commission investigated the grievances of the Arabs and found that the conflict

Founders of Degania, Palestine's first kibbutz, pose for a photograph at their primitive farming settlement. Arab farmers were often displaced when Jewish settlers purchased land to build their kibbutzim.

inspired all Arabs with the hope of reviving in a free and united Arab world the traditions of the Arab golden age. The Jews similarly are inspired by their historic past. They mean to show what the Jewish nation can achieve when restored to the land of its birth. National assimilation between Arabs and Jews is thus ruled out.

Having decided that Jews and Arabs could not share the same land peacefully, the commission recommended partition—dividing the region of Palestine into an Arab state and a Jewish state. The Zionists accepted the idea, but the Arabs rejected it.

The Arab rebellion against the British was not put down until 1938, after 101 British soldiers, 463 Jews, and an estimated 5,000 Arabs had been killed and the commission's plan for partition had been dropped. An uneasy quiet followed.

Palestinian snipers are arrested and taken into custody by British police officers during the 1938 Arab rebellion. Arabs used sniping to protest both the British rule and Jewish immigration.

World War II

By 1939 it was clear that war in Europe was again imminent. Keeping peace in Palestine meant a large commitment of British troops, something the British could not afford while fighting a war. Further, the British wanted to avoid antagonizing other Arab states who might support Germany. After a failed attempt to negotiate peace between the Arabs and Jews in Palestine, Britain decided to back down on the promises it made in the Balfour Declaration of a Jewish state in Palestine. In 1939, Britain issued a government policy statement declaring 1) that Palestine would not be a Jewish state, 2) that Jewish immigration to Palestine would be strictly limited, and 3) that Jewish immigration would be stopped completely after five years. The British further announced that in ten years they would create an independent state of Palestine as a whole, with Jews and Arabs enjoying equal rights.

The Zionists saw the British declaration as a betrayal. Limiting Jewish immigration meant that Jews would remain a small minority in an Arab-controlled Palestine. The Jews would still be at the mercy of a non-Jewish government and a non-Jewish majority population—a condition that had existed in Europe for centuries.

Nevertheless, the Palestinian Jews fought alongside the British against the Nazis. By 1944 the Nazi defeat was inevitable, and the Jews were ready to again take up their fight for a Jewish state. Menachem Begin, who was then the head of a radical underground military group called the Irgun, an offshoot of the Haganah, called for an end to British occupation of Palestine:

> There is no longer any armistice between the Jewish people and the British Administration in [the land of Israel] which hands our brothers over to Hitler. . . . This, then is our demand: immediate transfer of power in Eretz Israel to a Provisional Hebrew government.

2

Israel and Its Enemies

WHEN WORLD WAR II ended, Nazi atrocities against the Jews were revealed. The world was horrified to learn that six million European Jews—one-third of the world's Jewish population—had been murdered. The Jews in Palestine became more determined than ever to establish a Jewish state, and they won international support for their aims. The British were pressured to allow more Jews to immigrate to Palestine. However, at the same time, the Arabs warned that they would not tolerate a Jewish state in Palestine.

Many Jews were determined to use whatever means necessary to achieve a Jewish state. In July 1946 members of the Irgun bombed the King David Hotel in Jerusalem, which contained the offices of the British administration. Eighty-eight people were killed. Meanwhile, the Haganah was attempting to illegally transport Jewish refugees from Europe into Palestine. Britain remained firm in its policy against Jewish immigration and turned back the ships it intercepted. One such ship, the *Exodus*, was intercepted by the British in July 1947. The British ordered the *Exodus* back to the port in southern France from which it had sailed, but the four thousand Jews aboard refused to disembark there. The *Exodus* was then sent to the port of Hamburg, Germany, where its passengers were removed by force. Newspapers around the world carried the story of the *Exodus*, criticizing the British for its inhumane treatment of the Jews.

British rescue workers scour the rubble of the King David Hotel following its bombing in July 1946. Members of the Irgun, a radical Jewish group, claimed responsibility for the explosion, which killed eighty-eight people.

The tense situation between Britain and the Jews and the Arabs continued to escalate. Jews, whose population had increased to about one-third the population of Palestine, insisted on an independent state. The Arabs continued to oppose partition of Palestine. Finally, the British gave up. Tired of war and worried that its interests in the Middle East would be endangered if it met its promise to the Jews, Britain announced that "their rule has proved to be unworkable in practice, [and] the obligations

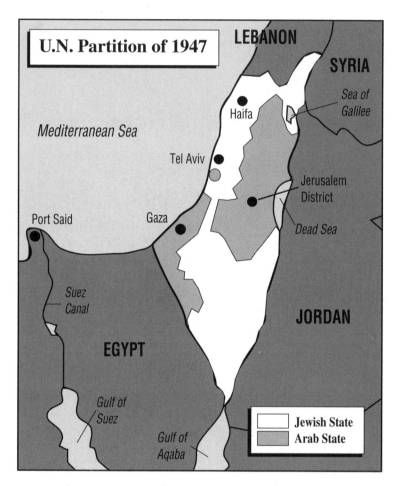

U.N. Partition of 1947

LEBANON

SYRIA

Sea of Galilee

Haifa

Mediterranean Sea

Tel Aviv

Jerusalem District

Port Said

Gaza

Dead Sea

Suez Canal

JORDAN

EGYPT

Gulf of Suez

Gulf of Aqaba

☐ Jewish State
▨ Arab State

undertaken to the two communities [Jews and Arabs] [are] irreconcilable."

The British then turned the problem over to the United Nations to resolve. In November 1947 the United Nations announced a partition plan for Palestine. Fifty-seven percent of the land would be allotted to a Jewish state, and the balance to an Arab state, with Jerusalem under the control of the United Nations because of its religious significance to Jews, Christians, and Muslims. As they had in 1937, the Arabs refused to accept a plan that gave away land they considered to be theirs. Fighting broke out immediately between Jews and Arabs. Britain announced that it would begin to pull out of Palestine on May 15, 1948. The stage was set for a bloody struggle.

The birth of Israel

When the partition was announced, Arabs began attacking Jewish settlements and terrorizing Jewish sections of larger towns. Zionists knew they must act quickly to protect themselves and to occupy and control the land granted to them under the partition. Fighting intensified. On Christmas Day 1947 more than a hundred Arabs and Jews were killed. The Haganah and two Jewish extremist groups, the Stern Gang and the Irgun, launched attacks against Arabs, driving them from their villages. In the most notorious raid, the Irgun attacked the Arab village of Deir Yassin, killing 254 men, women, and children.

Unlike the Jews, who had no foreign armies to help in their fight, the Palestinian Arabs did not fight alone. In 1945 the Arab states of Egypt, Syria, Iraq, Saudi Arabia, Yemen, and Transjordan had formed the Arab League to stop Zionism. Some members of the Arab League simply wanted to save Palestine for the Palestinian Arabs; others wanted to push the Jews into the sea. All rejected Israel's right to exist. As the deadline for British withdrawal approached, the Arab League was poised for attack.

When the United Nations failed to end the hostilities between Jews and Arabs in Palestine, Britain announced its withdrawal from the war-torn region.

On May 14, 1948, as British soldiers began to pull out of Palestine, David Ben-Gurion, Israel's first prime minister, made a historic announcement: "We . . . do hereby proclaim the establishment of the Jewish State in the Land of Israel—the State of Israel."

For the Jews, it was a time of great celebration, coming just three years after the close of World War II and the liberation of the terrible Nazi concentration camps. Many of the new Israeli citizens were refugees from the Nazi death camps. The dream of Theodor Herzl, founder of Zionism—that Jews form an independent Jewish state to allow them freedom from persecution—had been fulfilled.

But the celebration of the birth of Israel was short-lived; on May 15, 1948, just hours after Ben-Gurion's proclamation, thirty thousand troops from five Arab countries—Jordan, Syria, Lebanon, Egypt, and Iraq—invaded Palestine on four fronts. The Israelis were heavily outnumbered, but fought desperately and managed to hold on to areas of Jewish Palestine. A four-week UN truce was called on June 11, during which British troops were able to com-

After being liberated from the Nazi concentration camps (pictured) at the close of World War II, many of the survivors immigrated to Palestine. The creation of Israel symbolized a victory for Jews around the world and fulfilled the Zionist dream of an independent Jewish state.

pletely evacuate the region. The truce no doubt saved the new Israeli state by giving it time to obtain additional arms from its supporters in the United States and in Europe.

Weakened Arab forces, on the other hand, suffered from a shortage of supplies and were quarreling among themselves. When the fighting began again on July 7, the Israelis had the upper hand.

A lasting solution?

A new truce was arranged by the United Nations ten days later. UN negotiator Count Bernadotte of the Swedish Red Cross suggested a lasting solution to the conflict: The Negev desert in southern Palestine would be given to the Arabs, the region of western Galilee in northern Palestine to the Jews. David Ben-Gurion was ready to accept the proposal, even though some Israeli forces were cut off in the Negev desert, and there was no guarantee they could be rescued. However, radical groups within the Israeli military refused to accept the solution. On September 19, Count Bernadotte and the French UN observer in Jerusalem were assassinated, many believed by these radical elements. Ben-Gurion, realizing Israel would be condemned by the world for the assassinations, disarmed the radicals and jailed two hundred of them.

Fighting resumed in October, after Israel had been resupplied with additional arms from its supporters in other countries. Once resupplied, Ben-Gurion was ready to fight for Negev. This time the Israelis were more successful. Fearful that the United Nations would insist that they surrender the Negev to the Arabs, they attacked Egyptian forces in the desert region, rescuing their own stranded fighters. The Israelis then captured Egyptian territory in the Sinai, a mountainous, mineral-rich peninsula at Israel's

David Ben-Gurion, Israel's first prime minister, carefully guided the young state. However, Ben-Gurion encountered resistance from militant Israeli groups who disliked his attempts to resolve conflicts with the Arabs.

Arabs were driven from their homes when Israel gained control of the Negev and the Sinai. Displaced men, women, and children formed refugee camps (pictured) in neighboring Arab countries.

southern tip. In the north, they pushed the Arab forces out of Galilee and occupied part of Lebanon.

Israel's success forced the Egyptians to sue for peace. On February 24, 1949, Israel and Egypt signed an armistice that gave Israel the Negev, but Egypt retained a piece of southern coastal area around Gaza, which was later known as the Gaza Strip. Agreements with Lebanon, Jordan, and Syria were signed in the following months, and Israel withdrew its forces from Lebanon. Land on the western bank of the Jordan River that encompassed the regions of Nablus in the north and Hebron in the south came under Jordanian control, and the region became known as the West Bank. But the armistice agreements brought merely a temporary halt to war, not permanent peace. The Arab states still refused to acknowledge Israel's right to exist.

Palestinian refugees

In the end, Israel had gained more territory than had originally been granted it by the UN partition—approximately 77 percent of the land of Palestine. By refusing to accept the original UN partition plan and opting instead for war, the Arabs had lost their chance for a Palestinian state. About 160,000 Palestinian Arabs remained in Israeli territory under Israeli rule, but by the end of 1949 approximately 800,000 more were refugees, driven from their homes in land now occupied by Israel, and living in refugee camps in surrounding Arab countries. For thousands of young Palestinian Arabs, the refugee camps would be the only home they would ever know. The Palestinians call this massive loss of home and land simply "the Catastrophe."

The United Nations attempted to help the refugees settle permanently in other Arab countries, but the Palestinians refused the UN aid. Fawaz Turki, a Palestinian writer who grew up in the refugee camps, explains why:

> We wanted nothing short of returning to our homeland. And from Syria, Lebanon and Jordan, we would see, a few miles, a few yards, across the border, a land where we had been born, where we had lived, and where we felt the earth. "This is my land," we would shout, or cry, or sing, or plead, or reason.

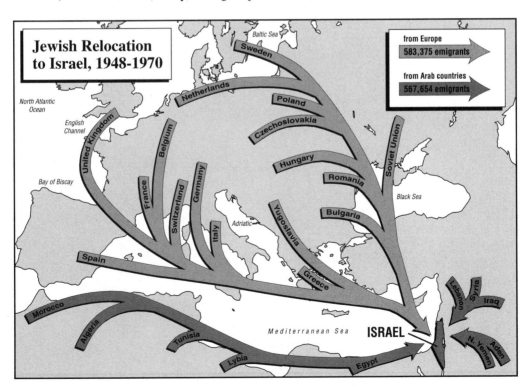

Jewish Relocation to Israel, 1948-1970

from Europe
583,375 emigrants

from Arab countries
567,654 emigrants

In the years that followed, Israel energetically went about building a nation. New immigrants flooded into the country, doubling the population in just four years. Western countries and wealthy Jewish communities abroad financed the building of new towns, settlements, and roads. To help people of different languages and cultures become part of the new nation, the ancient biblical language of Hebrew was taught to new immigrants. Always conscious of threats to its borders, the government required all citizens, men and women alike, to spend some time in military service.

The State of Israel was taking shape, and with memories of the Holocaust still painfully fresh, the Israelis were determined to survive even under threat of annihilation by the Arab world. Israelis were acutely aware that they were a very small state surrounded by enemies, tens of millions of Arabs, who had boasted that they would push the Jews into the sea. The Israelis knew that, unlike Arab nations, they could not afford to lose a war. If an Arab nation lost a war to Israel, Arab forces could retreat, lick their wounds, regroup, and rearm. However, if Israel were to lose a war, Israelis had nowhere to go. To lose could mean destruction of the State of Israel, something the Israelis were determined to prevent. Consequently, they spent great energy developing armed forces. Though costly and nerve-racking, this siege mentality helped form Israel into a cohesive nation.

Surrounded by hostile Arab neighbors, Israelis were forced to develop their armed forces. The military unified Israelis and helped them to fend off Arab attacks that threatened to destroy their young nation.

When Egyptian president Gamal Abdel Nasser (pictured) seized possession of the Suez Canal, he started the Suez War of 1956. Although Great Britain, France, and Israel joined forces, they failed to defeat Nasser.

Over the next two and a half decades Israel and its Arab neighbors went to war four times. The first conflict was the Suez War of 1956. Early that year Egyptian president Gamal Abdel Nasser declared the Suez Canal, linking the Red Sea and the Mediterranean, to be the property of Egypt. The canal had been built and owned by foreign investors, mainly Great Britain and France; now both European powers retaliated against Nasser's act by signing a secret agreement with the Israelis to invade Egypt and help regain control of the Suez Canal. In October 1956, Israeli troops invaded the Sinai. Then, according to their secret deal, Britain and France landed troops near Suez and publicly demanded that Israel and Egypt both withdraw their forces to ten miles on either side of the canal. The plan was that Britain and France would then move in and take control of the Suez Canal. However, when Nasser refused to withdraw and rendered the canal unusable by blocking it with sunken ships, the plan failed. The United Nations demanded a cease-fire. Ultimately, British, French, and Israeli troops withdrew, after a loss of two hundred Israeli and three thousand Egyptian lives.

The Six-Day War of 1967 would have the most far-reaching consequences for Israel and the Palestinian Arabs.

Israeli forces patrol the streets of Jerusalem after capturing the city from Jordan. At the close of the Six-Day War, Israel acquired land from Egypt, Syria, and Jordan, greatly expanding its territories.

Since 1948, Palestinian Arab guerrilla fighters who lived in exile had continued to attack Israeli settlements. President Nasser of Egypt continued to call for Arab unity and made fiery speeches threatening to "liberate Palestine," meaning to destroy Israel. When Arab nations joined forces and began a military buildup, Israel decided to strike first. On June 5, 1967, Israeli planes attacked Egyptian airfields, destroying the Egyptian air force on the ground. Just hours later, the Israelis struck Jordanian, Syrian, and Iraqi airfields. By the end of the first day, Israel had achieved air supremacy. In fierce fighting, Israel thoroughly defeated Egyptian, Jordanian, and Syrian forces before agreeing to a UN-sponsored cease-fire six days later.

The war ends

At the end of the Six-Day War, the territory controlled by Israel was greatly expanded: Israelis occupied the Sinai and the Gaza Strip (formerly controlled by Egypt), the Golan Heights (formerly controlled by Syria), and East Jerusalem and all of the West Bank (formerly controlled by Jordan). About 1.8 million Arabs now lived in lands controlled by Israelis, and another 200,000 Palestinians had fled.

Not only had the war failed to destroy Israel and gain a Palestinian homeland as the Arab nations had hoped, the Gaza Strip and the West Bank, once designated for the Palestinians, had been lost. East Jerusalem, designated by the United Nations as under international jurisdiction, was officially annexed by, or made a permanent part of, Israel, and East Jerusalem citizens, who were mostly Arabs, became Israeli citizens. Despite the urging of the United Nations, Israel refused to withdraw without concessions from the territories it had captured, claiming it needed the lands as a buffer to protect it from its enemies.

The humiliating defeat of the Arab nations, and Israel's expansion into what Palestinian Arabs felt should be their land, further fueled the anger and hatred of Arab nations and Palestinian Arabs against Israel. For its part, Israel offered to return control of much of the territory seized during the Six-Day War if the Arabs would make peace and officially recognize Israel's right to exist. The United Nations made the same offer in the form of Resolution 242, which called for

> I) withdrawal of Israeli armed forces from territories occupied in the recent conflict;

> II) termination of all claims or states of belligerency and respect for and acknowledgement of the sovereignty, territorial integrity, and political independence of every state in the area and their right to live in peace within secure and recognized boundaries free from threats or acts of force.

The Arabs refused the offer and declared that they would not make peace, would not negotiate, and would not recognize Israel as a legitimate state.

The Yom Kippur War

In reaction to the humiliation of the Six-Day War, Egypt began a military buildup and launched commando raids on Israel designed to keep Israel on edge; Israel retaliated in kind. The war of attrition—a gradual wearing down—continued until 1970, when Israel and Egypt agreed to a cease-fire proposed by the United States. The cease-fire lasted three years.

Mourners gather in a military cemetery to bury soldiers who died during the 1973 Yom Kippur War. Some 2,800 Israelis were killed and another 8,000 were wounded when Egyptian forces launched a surprise attack on the Jewish holiday.

In 1973, hoping to regain its prestige in the Arab world, Egypt once again launched a war against Israel. The day chosen for the surprise attack was the Jewish holiday Yom Kippur, or the Day of Atonement, which fell on October 6. Israel, unprepared for war, suffered enormous casualties proportionate to its small size—2,800 dead and 8,000 wounded. Although Arab losses were much higher—more than 20,000 dead and 60,000 wounded—as a percentage Israel's losses were equivalent to more than twice the U.S. losses in Vietnam in ten years. Despite the heavy casualties inflicted by the surprise attack, the Israelis managed to marshal their forces and launch a successful counterattack. The Soviet Union, which had been arming and supporting the Arab states, threatened to intervene, which would have forced the United States to come to Israel's defense. However, negotiations between the United States and the Soviet Union finally led to a cease-fire on October 23, 1973.

Peace would be a long time coming, however. Arab nations were no longer as willing to go to war with Israel, but Palestinian Arabs were not ready for peace. They were more determined than ever to found a Palestinian state, and they were prepared to use whatever means necessary to achieve their goal.

3

Arafat and the PLO

DURING THE 1960s several militant Palestinian groups emerged whose aim was to unite the Palestinians scattered across the Middle East. Disappointed in the failure of the Arab governments to destroy Israel and win a Palestinian homeland, these groups were determined to rely on their own efforts to achieve their goal. Some factions, such as the Popular Front for the Liberation of Palestine (PFLP) and the Democratic Front for the Liberation of Palestine (DFLP), were heavily influenced by the writings of Karl Marx, whose theories influenced the communist revolution in Russia. To them, liberation meant not just destroying Israel, but bringing about revolution in the moderate Arab states as well.

The largest and most influential of these groups was called Fatah, an Arabic word meaning "conquest" or "victory," and one of its founders was Yasir Arafat. Unlike other groups, Fatah's sole aim was to establish a Palestinian state. Fatah called on young men to become guerrilla fighters, or fedayeen, literally "men of sacrifice." Groups of fedayeen began launching guerrilla raids against Israeli territories and citizens.

The beginnings of the PLO

Some Arab governments disapproved of the guerrilla raids against Israel. Fedayeen activities threatened to force them into another war to help the Palestinians, for which they were not ready. In 1964 Nasser called a meeting of the Arab League and urged the establishment of the Palestine

Yasir Arafat (pictured) helped found Fatah, a militant Palestinian group whose goal was to establish a Palestinian state. Fatah used guerrilla warfare, launching raids in Israel and against its citizens.

Liberation Organization (PLO). Nasser wanted to give Palestinians around the Middle East the sense that something was being done to address their grievances and give them a voice. He also wanted to keep the unruly Palestinian guerrilla fighters under his control, so that they would not force the Arab world into a war they did not want to fight.

The stated purpose of the PLO was to destroy Israel and to establish a Palestinian homeland. The Palestine Liberation Organization comprised the Palestinian National Council of 422 Palestinian representatives chosen by Arab governments, a president elected by the council (actually handpicked by Nasser) and executive and military branches, the Executive Council, and the Palestine Liberation Army. The PLO Covenant, or charter, declaring its principles was adopted on June 1, 1964. The charter claimed that "Palestine is an Arab homeland," and Article 19 of the charter stated that

> partition of Palestine in 1947 and the establishment of the state of Israel are entirely illegal, regardless of the passage of time, because they were contrary to the will of the Palestinian people and to their natural right in their homeland.

In other words, the charter claimed that Israel had no right to exist.

Arafat and Fatah boycotted the organization, labeling it a tool of Arab states who would not act to help Palestinians against their own interests. However, the majority of the Palestinians supported the PLO, believing it gave them a voice and an army to fight for them. Many Fatah supporters went over to the PLO, and Fatah had trouble raising funds.

Two men stop to read flyers outside of a Palestine Liberation Organization (PLO) recruitment office. The PLO was established in 1964 by President Nasser and the Arab League to destroy Israel and create a Palestinian state.

Fatah leaders never wavered, however. Following the 1967 Six-Day War and Israel's occupation of the West Bank, Fatah stepped up terrorist raids against Israel. Ultimately, Fatah's fortunes improved following an incident just across the Jordan River from the West Bank, in the small town of Karameh. The villagers of Karameh, incensed by the death and destruction caused by Israeli shelling during the Six-Day War, had invited Fatah fedayeen to use their town as a base from which to launch raids against Israel. The fedayeen planted land mines and explosives in Israeli civilian territory. In March 1968 one person was killed and twenty-eight injured when an Israeli school bus hit a Fatah bomb. Finally, Israel was determined to clear out the fedayeen in Karameh and planned an attack against the town, warning the civilians to leave. A Fatah commander (Arafat claims it was he) gave a stirring speech urging the fighters to take a stand against Israel. A force of less than three hundred stood up against Israeli tanks and fifteen hundred troops, with no hope of winning, but they fought so desperately that the Israelis were forced to withdraw briefly. The Israelis finally overran the village and Fatah retreated, but Yasir Arafat and Fatah gained a reputation for courage against Israel. Arafat became a Palestinian hero, Fatah merged with the PLO, and Arafat eventually gained control of the organization he had once boycotted. He was elected its chairman in 1969.

Operating from bases first in Jordan and then in Lebanon, Arafat stepped up his campaign of terror against Israel. He grew enormously popular with the Palestinian people, who considered him their leader and the representative voice of the Palestinian people. In 1988, the Palestinian writer Fawaz Turki explained that Palestinians loved Arafat because he represented the essence of their common experience:

> He is the essential Palestinian Everyman, living a more authentically Palestinian lifestyle than any of them—no family, no home, no passport, no country, no property, consumed by Palestine and nothing else.

A young Palestinian proudly carries a poster of Yasir Arafat during a PLO rally. Arafat's efforts against the Israelis made him a popular hero to the Palestinian people.

Following the Yom Kippur War of 1973, Arafat and other PLO leaders began to realize guerrilla warfare gained them little. They finally accepted that it might be impossible to defeat Israel militarily. Negotiating with Israel for a Palestinian state composed of Gaza and the West Bank might be the more practical path. But there were pitfalls to that strategy.

When Arafat was elected PLO chairman in 1969, he immediately began to bring other fedayeen groups into the

PLO. This policy increased the PLO's size and resources, but also made it more difficult to control. Groups within the PLO did not necessarily support all of the PLO's positions. An Israeli professor of international relations describes the PLO this way:

> In effect, the PLO was in 1967–70—and has remained to date—a loose, voluntary confederation in which the militants (who are often in the service of one or another Arab government) basically call the shots.

Consequently, when Arafat started to talk about settling for less than the whole of Palestine, the more radical groups were outraged. They still advocated armed conflict to destroy Israel and establish a Palestinian state, no matter what the cost. However, Arafat became convinced that it was time to try peaceful means to resolve the issue.

Talk of giving up the struggle for all of Palestine finally caused a break in the PLO. Arafat and Fatah continued to argue for diplomacy while radical PLO groups, supported by extremist Arab states such as Syria and Iraq, continued to use guerrilla and terrorist tactics in Israel and in other countries in hopes of gaining all of Palestine.

The PLO and terrorism

Arafat was unable to control the terrorist elements of the PLO, who launched attacks on targets around the world, hoping to bring the plight of the Palestinians to the world's attention. And Israel did not trust Arafat's condemnation of Palestinian terrorist attacks; Israeli intelligence believed Arafat continued to oversee guerrilla attacks on Israel by Fatah fighters based in Lebanon.

Whether Arafat directly approved them or not, the attacks continued. In May 1974 terrorists held a hundred teenagers and five teachers hostage at a school in northern Israel. In the end, twenty-two people were killed and fifty-six others were wounded by the Palestinians when Israeli forces stormed the school. Israel retaliated by bombing PLO strongholds in Lebanon, killing fifty people and injuring another two hundred. In 1978 a Palestinian attack on a bus near the Israeli city of Tel Aviv killed thirty-three

Israelis. In 1980 six Israelis were killed and sixteen others were wounded by Palestinian terrorists who machine-gunned worshipers at a synagogue in Hebron. Also in 1980 Palestinian terrorists slipped into an Israeli settlement at night, capturing several young children. In the end, one child was killed and five were wounded.

Finally, in June 1982, Israel launched an all-out attack on the PLO bases in Lebanon. Ninety thousand Israeli troops laid siege to PLO strongholds. U.S. intermediaries were involved in cease-fire negotiations, and finally the PLO leaders agreed to leave Lebanon after the United States guaranteed the safety of the Palestinian refugee camps. After PLO guerrillas left, Lebanese Christian militia, autonomous military groups with bitter religious and political enmity toward the Palestinian refugees, entered Palestinian refugee camps in areas controlled by Israel. In the following two days, the militia murdered and mutilated the bodies of more than seven hundred men, women, and children,

In 1982, Israel bombarded PLO strongholds in Lebanon, forcing its citizens to run for cover as buildings crumbled around their feet.

while Israeli soldiers stood by under orders not to interfere. The PLO felt betrayed by the United States, which had promised the safety of the Palestinian civilians. The world was outraged, including many Israeli citizens who called for an investigation of Israel's part in the matter.

Following the disaster in Lebanon, the PLO forces scattered throughout the Arab world, and the PLO itself splintered into three main groups: the remnants of Arafat's Fatah; a group loyal to the PFLP, which called for social revolution and armed fighting; and an anti-Arafat group of radical terrorists backed by Syria, Iraq, and Libya. These countries hoped to gain control of a future Palestinian nation. The most radical group, led by Abu Nidal, tried to assassinate Arafat because of his so-called traitorous actions in discussing peace with Israel. They missed Arafat but did succeed in assassinating some top PLO officials loyal to him. Arafat and Fatah seemed near collapse; Arafat was hunted by militant Islamic groups as well as Israeli agents. Arab governments such as Syria and Iraq had turned against him. Syrian president Hafez al-Assad wanted to gain control of the PLO by putting the PLO factions loyal

Yasir Arafat listens as a Lebanese woman tells him about the damage caused to her home during the Israeli air raid.

A guerrilla fighter gives the victory sign during PLO training exercises. Despite divisions within the PLO, Yasir Arafat remained a popular leader

to him in the top PLO spots; Iraq's Saddam Hussein had similar ambitions and was equipping fedayeen groups who opposed Arafat.

Many people believed that the power of the PLO and Yasir Arafat had finally been destroyed, but as always, Arafat managed to regroup. He set up headquarters in Tunis, Tunisia, then seat of the Arab League. From Tunis he directed the small groups of Fatah fedayeen who maintained a foothold in Syria and Lebanon. Arafat and his top aides lived like fugitives, sleeping every night in a different house to avoid being detected by the Israeli and Palestinian assassins who hunted them.

Despite the splintering within the PLO, Arafat, with his remarkable skills of persuasion and negotiation, managed to regain the support of many PLO members. At the 1984 meeting of the Palestinian National Council, Arafat gained enough votes to retain chairmanship of the PLO. Arafat's continued chairmanship meant that a negotiated peace settlement between the Israelis and the Palestinians was still a possibility. However, many of the militant groups who opposed peace talks remained a disruptive force in the organization, assuring that peace would not come easily.

4

A Historic Agreement

As THE DECADE of the 1990s arrived, the Israelis and the Palestinians were still in constant conflict. After more than forty years, Palestinians were no closer to their own homeland. The Israelis were no closer to a lasting peace. Aging leaders of both Israel and the PLO were growing weary, and they realized that the use of force or violence brought them no closer to resolution. Nevertheless, these factors might not have led to a historic agreement had the world not been undergoing some dramatic changes.

A changing world

Several world events finally tipped the scales toward peace in the Middle East. First was the 1991 breakup of the Soviet Union. The Middle East had long been a battleground in the cold war between the United States and the Soviet Union, with the Soviets backing the Arab nations and the United States backing Israel. With the Soviet Union's collapse, neither the PLO nor Arab countries such as Syria could continue to count on the Soviets for arms and financial support. Israel, too, had lost some of the unconditional support of the United States and was faced with an ever-increasing burden of supporting its state-of-the-art military.

Realignment of Arab states also spurred the peace process. Egypt had signed a formal peace treaty with Israel in 1979. Now other Arab nations, such as Jordan and Lebanon, seemed ready to give up their long and costly

fight with Israel. The Palestinians now faced the prospect of abandonment by the Arab states that had supported their cause for so long.

The Palestinians also feared the growing number of Israeli settlements in the occupied territories of Gaza and the West Bank, which Israel had captured during the 1967 Six-Day War. Palestinians saw the settlements as a sign that Israel intended to keep the occupied territories. Building settlements on the West Bank was in direct opposition to UN Resolution 242, passed at the end of the 1967 war, which was to be the basis for resolving the conflict between Palestinians and Israelis: Israel would return the land it had occupied in 1967 in return for peace and recognition of its right to exist. When the United States urged Israel to stop building settlements in occupied territory, right-wing Israeli politician Yitzhak Shamir announced, "All of our territories that can be built on will be populated by Jews up to the horizon's edge."

During the Camp David summit in 1979, Egyptian president Anwar Sadat (left) and Israeli prime minister Menachem Begin (right) worked out a peace treaty with the help of U.S. president Jimmy Carter.

In 1977, when conservative Menachem Begin came to power in Israel, there were 36 outposts with 5,000 settlers in the occupied territories. By 1990 there were 120 settlements, with about 70,000 settlers. While some Israeli government officials wanted settlements in the occupied territories for political reasons, many of the settlers had religious reasons for being there. As one West Bank settler explained: "Jewish people come here not because of political reasons, not because of security reasons, but because this land was promised to them by the Lord."

Another international conflict indirectly influenced Israel's participation in the peace process. During the 1991 Persian Gulf War, sparked by Iraq's invasion of its tiny neighbor Kuwait, the United States and Arab and European allies drove Iraqi forces out of Kuwait. While Israel did not participate directly in the fighting, it quickly found it was highly vulnerable to the sophisticated and deadly new weaponry of the war. Iraqi Scud missiles launched

Iraqi Scud missiles ripped through Israeli cities during the 1991 Persian Gulf War. In Tel Aviv (pictured), Israelis lived in fear while bombs devastated parts of their city.

hundreds of miles away hit apartment buildings in Israeli cities. Frightened Israeli citizens were on constant alert, fearing poison gas attacks by Iraqi artillery. Many called for a peaceful resolution of the conflict, and a reduction in Middle Eastern hostilities in general.

The Gulf War proved to be a turning point for the PLO, which found itself weakened because it backed the wrong side in the war. The tiny state of Kuwait had enormous oil wealth and had been a generous financial supporter of the PLO. When Iraq invaded Kuwait, Arafat sided with Iraq, perhaps because Iraq had always been Israel's sworn enemy. When Iraq was forced to withdraw from Kuwait, the PLO found itself without the substantial financial support it had enjoyed from Kuwait and from Saudi Arabia, who had also opposed Iraq. This disadvantage, which Israel no doubt perceived, put pressure on the PLO to negotiate with Israel.

The *intifada*

Perhaps the most dramatic episode forcing Israel and the Palestinians to seek peace was the *intifada*, or uprising. While Arafat was fighting the battle for Palestine from other countries, the daily lives of Palestinians in the occupied territories remained miserable. Israeli occupation was harsh, sometimes brutal.

In December 1987, the Israelis and the PLO were both caught by surprise with an uprising of Palestinians living in the occupied territories. For twenty years Palestinians in Gaza and the West Bank had lived under Israeli occupation. They had no rights as citizens, no representation in the government, and yet they were expected to pay taxes to Israel, taxes that paid the Israeli troops who occupied their towns.

The uprising was not organized by well-trained guerrilla fighters in other countries. It sprang from the people themselves. Beginning as a spontaneous demonstration against the rumored killing of four Palestinians by an Israeli military truck, the movement quickly spread throughout the occupied territories and drew immediate grassroots

In December 1987, Palestinians living in Gaza and the West Bank staged an intifada, *or uprising, to protest Israeli occupation. These Palestinian youths aid the uprising by building a barricade of burning tires under a banner welcoming visitors to Gaza.*

support. The "soldiers" of the *intifada* were mostly youths who harassed the Israelis by throwing rocks at Israeli patrols, setting up barricades of burning tires, displaying PLO flags in defiance of Israeli military orders, and painting nationalist slogans on buildings.

The Israelis responded quickly and harshly to the ongoing campaign. In the first year of the *intifada*, almost twenty thousand Palestinians were arrested and more than three hundred were killed by the Israelis. Since most of the militants were minors, Israeli authorities closed the schools and enforced strict curfews. Palestinians consider themselves among the best educated of Arabs and they highly value education, so the school closings—including the closing of universities—was an especially hard blow.

Meanwhile, the PLO, now headquartered in Tunis, quickly moved to take advantage of the *intifada*, funneling money into the territories and using propaganda and financial aid to attempt to control *intifada* activities. The PLO wanted the Palestinians to use nonviolent methods to gain world attention and sympathy for their cause, fearing that violence would bring harsh criticism. However, the new, younger generation of Palestinians was not easily controlled. These youths believed the PLO, in its distant headquarters, had grown soft and lost its will to fight. Other more militant groups began to challenge the PLO leadership.

A new group emerged out of the *intifada*—Hamas, a radical Islamic fundamentalist group that vowed to pursue a holy war to establish a state based on Islamic law, like the country of Iran. Hamas gained popular support—and when their support was not spontaneous, Hamas intimidated

many Palestinians, sometimes kidnapping and murdering them. By 1991 Hamas had become a serious threat to the Israelis. Israel began to realize that it might be better to make peace with the more moderate PLO than to try to control or live beside 1.5 million Palestinians committed to the goals and tactics of Hamas.

The first steps

In 1991 the United States organized peace talks between Israel and the Arab states of Syria, Lebanon, Jordan, Egypt, Saudi Arabia, and Palestinian representatives. The talks ran into problems before they began. Prime Minister Yitzhak Shamir of Israel insisted that Israel would not negotiate with any representatives from the PLO. Israel considered Arafat and the PLO bloody terrorists who attacked and murdered innocent civilians. On the other hand, Palestinians insisted that the PLO was the legitimate representative of the Palestinian people. Arafat told Western news reporters: "We have said yes to a peace conference and we do not post conditions . . . but we are not bending to Israeli conditions."

A young Hamas supporter leads a procession during a rally for the controversial Islamic group. Members of Hamas have vowed to fight a holy war to establish an Islamic state.

Peace talks dragged on for nearly two years, but peace seemed a hopeless dream.

A private peace

Just when the peace talks seemed to be mired in insurmountable disagreements, a break came. In 1992 Israel elected a new prime minister, Yitzhak Rabin, the general during the 1967 Six-Day War who had captured the new territories for Israel. Rabin, politically more moderate than Shamir, was willing to make some concessions for peace. Like Arafat, Rabin was growing older and was beginning to desire a legacy of peace. As one of Rabin's aides explained: "As the one who brought all the territories to Israel, and as a symbol of war in Israel, he personally wants to enter history as a hero of both war and peace."

In 1992, Yitzhak Rabin became prime minister of Israel. Rabin, a former war hero, now worked to establish peace with his longtime enemy.

Official peace talks, organized by the United States in Washington, D.C., were going nowhere. The United States had arranged negotiations between Israel and moderate Palestinian leaders from Gaza and from the West Bank. According to Israeli wishes, the PLO was out of the negotiations altogether. It soon became clear, however, that the Palestinian delegates had little power to implement any agreements they might reach. A majority of Palestinians in the West Bank and Gaza remained loyal to the PLO, whose leaders were based in Tunis.

In the meantime, however, PLO influence with Palestinians in the occupied territories was beginning to decline, and Islamic fundamentalist groups such as Hamas and Islamic Jihad, which were financed by Iran, were drawing support once given to the PLO. The Israelis believed that Iran was developing nuclear weapons, and would soon pose a far greater threat to Israel than that

posed by the PLO. To Prime Minister Rabin and the Israelis, Arafat was becoming the lesser of two evils.

Terje Roed Larsen was a Norwegian social scientist engaged in research in the occupied territories. In June 1992, Larsen proposed opening a secret channel with moderate Palestinians and Israelis who supported peace. By late 1992, informal talks began in Norway. Israelis "didn't attach much importance to them," one source reports, but in the spring of 1993 the chief PLO negotiator presented the Israelis with a proposed agreement that served as a working base. Although many points needed further work, the PLO and Arafat agreed to concessions they had not been willing to make before. The most important concession was that the occupied territories would be handed over to Palestinian control a few regions at a time, rather than all at once.

Meetings were conducted in strict secrecy, as any concession made by PLO negotiators was sure to anger the radical elements in the PLO, possibly even resulting in an assassination attempt against PLO negotiators. Public disclosure of the negotiations would be sure to bring harsh criticism from both hard-line Israelis and militant Palestinians. Furthermore, the United States and other Arab countries might well be insulted at being left out of the negotiations. Israeli foreign minister Shimon Peres shuttled back and forth between Israel and Oslo personally delivering messages and keeping Prime Minister Rabin informed of progress.

A declaration of peace

Finally, Rabin endorsed the plan, and on August 20, 1993, Peres flew to Norway where he initialed the agreement, known officially as the Declaration of Principles on Palestinian Interim Self-Government Arrangements, which included the following provisions:

First, Palestinians would be given control of the Gaza Strip and the West Bank town of Jericho, and Israel would withdraw troops from those areas. One by one, other towns in the West Bank would be turned over to the Palestinians until the entire West Bank was under Palestinian control.

Israeli foreign minister Shimon Peres helped negotiate the monumental peace plan between Israel and Palestine.

Second, an elected Palestinian Council would govern the West Bank and Gaza. The council would be responsible for utilities, welfare agencies, and the police.

Third, Israel and the PLO would begin talks about control of the city of Jerusalem, the Israeli settlements on the West Bank, and the fate of Palestinian refugees who wished to return.

The agreement also stipulated that Israeli settlers were to be under the jurisdiction of Israel and that East Jerusalem would not be part of the self-governing area. Both sides agreed to continue negotiations to work out details of self-government in the West Bank.

Once these important points were agreed upon, the next step was to publicly announce the plan and obtain support from other countries, as well as from the Israeli and the Palestinian people, in preparation for the official signing of the peace accord. Before going public, however, on August 27, 1993, Rabin met with U.S. secretary of state Warren Christopher to explain the plan. Christopher was astonished, says one of his aides. "The scope of the agreement was stunning. This was now moving much faster than any of us had realized."

Criticism of the peace accord

When the plan was made public, Israeli opinion was split, 53 percent in favor and 45 percent opposed; 2 percent remained undecided. Of Palestinians surveyed in the occupied territories, 52.8 percent backed the plan. In Gaza and Jericho, regions from which Israelis would withdraw first, the approval rate was 70 percent and 75 percent, respectively.

The public announcement of the plan was immediately met with criticism. Many Israelis questioned how Israel could negotiate directly with the PLO, the bitter enemy that had vowed to destroy it. But as Prime Minister Rabin explained, "Peace is not made with friends. Peace is made with enemies."

Hastily arranged negotiations for the official signing of the peace accord hit a snag over the issue of mutual recognition. The PLO wanted Israel to recognize it as the official representative of the Palestinian people. Israel wanted the PLO to renounce terrorism and violence against Israel and to officially recognize its right to exist, fundamental issues of contention. However, both Rabin and Arafat knew that delaying the official signing would only give their critics time to organize perhaps violent opposition. Rabin and Arafat settled the issues—recognition for both sides—despite the fact that the Palestinian National Council had not yet repealed Article 19 of its charter, which stated that Israel had no right to exist. This issue would come up soon enough. Nevertheless, preparations began

for the final step—the official ceremony at which the parties would sign the accord.

Dancing in the streets

September 13, 1993, was the date selected for the official signing ceremony. The place was the lawn of the White House. Just three years earlier, no one would have predicted this historic event. An entire generation of Palestinians and Israelis had grown to adulthood hating and fearing each other. Israelis feared the PLO terrorist attacks launched against them in their own homes and around the world. Palestinians in refugee camps and in the occupied territories feared Israeli reprisals for such attacks, which often killed innocent women and children, just as the PLO had killed innocent women and children. The world could not imagine such bitterness could be set aside for peace. But Yitzhak Rabin stood before the world on the White

Government officials from Israel, the United States, and Palestine gather on the White House lawn for the signing of the Palestinian-Israeli peace accord.

House lawn and announced: "Enough of blood and tears. Enough."

As millions of people around the world watched the televised ceremony, Yasir Arafat extended his hand in peace to Yitzhak Rabin. Rabin accepted Arafat's handshake, thus ending more than twenty-five years of mortal enmity between the two. At the White House, many people wept as they watched. In the city of Jericho on the West Bank, thousands of Palestinians danced in the streets, waving Palestinian flags. In Jerusalem, huge crowds of Israelis cheered. Peace was at hand. President Bill Clinton gave voice to the hopes of millions when he addressed the Israelis and Palestinians on that day:

Yasir Arafat, Shimon Peres, and Yitzhak Rabin display the joint Nobel Peace Prize they were awarded in 1994.

> Together let us imagine what can be accomplished if all the energy and ability the Israelis and the Palestinians have invested into your struggle can now be channeled into cultivat-

ing the land and freshening the waters; into ending the boy-
cotts and creating new industry; into building a land as boun-
tiful and peaceful as it is holy.

For their work in promoting this remarkable step toward
peace in the Middle East, Israeli prime minister Yitzhak
Rabin, Israeli foreign minister Shimon Peres, and PLO
chairman Yasir Arafat shared the 1994 Nobel Peace Prize.
Their achievement notwithstanding, Amos Oz, Israeli nov-
elist and leader of an Israeli peace group, recalls the futil-
ity and waste of the years of conflict:

> After all, in the end, the Palestinians are only going to get a
> fraction of what they could have had with peace and honor
> back in 1948, forty-five years, five wars, and some 150,000
> deaths ago, ours as well as theirs. The Israelis, too, will get
> less than they could have had, had they been imaginative,
> generous, or even realistic back in 1967 and afterward. The
> dead will get nothing except for some wreaths and a flood of
> high-flown rhetoric.

5

Voices of Opposition

THOUGH A MAJORITY of Israelis endorsed the peace plan, even before the peace accord was signed, voices were raised in opposition. Many Israelis felt, first and foremost, that Arafat could not be trusted. They considered him an unrepentant murderer and a terrorist who, though he spoke peace, still secretly desired the destruction of Israel. Opponents pointed out that the Palestinian National Council had not yet removed the clauses in their charter that denied Israel's right to exist and that called for the destruction of Israel. (That language was not officially removed by the council until April 1996.) Many Israelis believed that Arafat was using the peace accord to strengthen the PLO's prestige among the Palestinians.

Furthermore, many Israelis believed that the establishment of independent Palestinian territories was a grave threat to Israeli security. Once established in secure bases on the West Bank and in Gaza, the PLO could easily strike at the heart of Israel. As Benjamin Netanyahu, a leader of the conservative Likud Party, said, "Saving the PLO from breaking apart and giving it a Palestinian state . . . will endanger the very existence of Israel." Many Israeli citizens expressed similar misgivings. Suri Orbach, a housewife and mother whose family moved to a small town on the West Bank in search of affordable housing, described her thoughts when the peace accord was signed in September 1993:

> We don't think this will bring us peace at all in the long run. We think in the long term, it is suicidal. A group of people

who are committed to our destruction is going to be given an area of land to become more powerful, and their aim is to destroy us. They can't even take [the PLO's vow to destroy Israel] out of their charter. How can they take it out of their hearts?

Another Israeli objection to the plan centered around the Israeli settlements on the West Bank. In ancient times the West Bank was known as Samaria and Judaea, the heart of ancient Jewish civilization. It was sacred ground to the ultraconservative Jews who settled in the area. They claimed that the land was given to them by God, eternally theirs by right. As rabbis claimed, the Torah, or Jewish scripture, directs the Jews to "populate the land of Israel." To give up the West Bank to Palestinians was unthinkable to the Jews who lived there. Consequently, the West Bank settlers made up the most determined opposition to the Palestinian-Israeli peace accord, flatly rejecting the

Citizens throughout Israel voiced their opposition to the peace agreement. In West Jerusalem, ultra right-wing Jews protested the plan by burning a poster calling Yitzhak Rabin "the traitor."

agreement's requirement that control of the West Bank be given to the Palestinians.

Israeli citizens voiced their opposition to the plan in various ways. Some were satisfied with simply displaying bumper sticker slogans denouncing Rabin. Others picketed the Israeli Knesset, or parliament, and some burned effigies of Rabin in public to show disapproval of the peace plan.

Jewish zealots and settlers in occupied territories

Other Israelis went much further in their opposition to the peace plan. When the accord was signed in September 1993, Rabin was labeled a traitor by angry Jewish zealots. Right-wing rabbis predicted that "a civil war . . . is likely to break out as a result of [the government's] dangerous and crazy steps." Though civil war did not materialize, violence did.

In February 1994, an Israeli settler in the West Bank, Baruch Goldstein, fired an assault rifle into a crowd of seven hundred Muslims at prayer in a holy shrine in the town of Hebron. Twenty-nine people lay dead before Goldstein was overpowered and killed by panicked and enraged worshipers. Goldstein represented some of the most militant of the Israeli settlers in the occupied territories. Of the 125,000 Israelis who settled in the occupied territories following 1967, about one-fourth were fierce militants who believed that the Jews were destined to take possession of their ancient holy land and drive out the Arabs. At the suggestion that the settlers might have to leave the territories, one settler in Hebron replied, "If I can't live in Hebron, you can't live in peace."

Voices of protest grew more shrill as Israeli troops began to pull out of the West Bank according to the terms of the peace agreement. In July 1995, Jewish settlers blocked the highways in the West Bank to protest the army's withdrawal. Worse yet, right-wing rabbis issued a religious ruling that called upon the Israeli soldiers to disobey their orders to pull out of the West Bank, although

In February 1994, Israeli Baruch Goldstein opened fire on the Muslim shrine in Hebron, killing twenty-nine worshipers.

few heeded their call. Foreign Minister Shimon Peres was outraged at the rabbis, saying, "What do they want, two peoples? One getting instructions from rabbis and the other living democratically?"

The assassination of Yitzhak Rabin

Amid increasing anger and hostility, another dramatic act of violence occurred on November 4, 1995. In the Israeli city of Tel Aviv–Jaffa, Prime Minister Yitzhak Rabin attended an evening peace rally, where more than a hundred thousand Israelis had gathered to support his efforts for peace. At the end of the rally, just as Rabin was about to step into his bulletproof Cadillac, a twenty-five-year-old man approached him from behind, reached between two security agents, and fired two bullets nearly point-blank into his back. Rabin died before morning.

Rabin's killer, who was immediately captured at the scene, was a former law student and religious zealot named Yigal Amir. He claimed he attacked Rabin because

An Arab man weeps beside the portrait of slain prime minister Yitzhak Rabin. Rabin was assassinated while attending a peace rally on November 4, 1995.

making peace with the Palestinians and giving up land to
them was a calamity for the Jews. Amir was tried and sentenced to life imprisonment in March 1996. Showing no
remorse at his trial, Amir said, "Everything I did, I did for
God, for the Torah of Israel, the people of Israel and the
land of Israel." Amir's actions and words demonstrated the
deep divisions within Israel over the peace accord.

From the moment of Rabin's death, accusations flew.
Rabin's widow, Leah, accused Rabin's political opponents
of tolerating the climate of violence that led to Rabin's
death. Right-wing Jewish rabbis were blamed for instigat-
ing the violence by suggesting that killing the prime minister could be justified under Jewish law. Violent
sentiment seemed to be everywhere, even in the religious
schools, as one rabbi—head of a religious school in
Jerusalem—explained:

> The students would ask the question—like they were asking
> what food should be eaten on the Sabbath—"Is it O.K. under
> Torah law [laws outlined in the Jewish holy books] to kill the
> Prime Minister?" Everyone was talking violence. There were
> hundreds like Amir.

Palestinian opposition

Many reasonable and thoughtful Palestinians disagreed
with the terms of peace as well. The Israelis supposedly
handed over authority in the Gaza Strip and in West Bank
towns to the PLO, but many alienated Palestinians felt that
Arafat and the PLO were little more than Israeli puppets.
Israel was no longer responsible for policing the newly autonomous regions; now the PLO was expected to do it. Israel no longer took responsibility for the roads, water
systems, hospitals, and so on, but if they chose they could
move their troops back into the occupied territories and
there was nothing the Palestinians could do about it.

Edward Said, a Palestinian intellectual and onetime
member of the Palestine National Council, broke with
Arafat during the Oslo peace negotiations. Said, once an
admirer of Arafat, protested, "The peace process made it
possible for the Israelis to hold on to Gaza and the West

Bank through indirect rule without any of the burden. . . . When the Israelis press the button, [Arafat] jumps."

Following the signing of the peace accord, many Palestinians became angry that the Jewish settlements on the West Bank were still expanding, which they saw as an act of bad faith on the part of the Israelis. The terms of peace stated that all West Bank territory would eventually come under Palestinian authority, and Israel seemed to disregard the agreement by allowing settlements to expand. Palestinians also became angry when the Israelis did not meet the agreed-upon timetable for turning over territory on the West Bank. What Israel saw as moving cautiously, the Palestinians saw as foot-dragging.

Some of the most vocal opposition to the peace plan came from within the PLO. When Arafat made peace with Israel, some dissident factions broke from the organization, vowing to continue the fight. These so-called rejectionist groups believed that by accepting autonomy rather than statehood and by recognizing Israel's right to exist and agreeing to live peacefully with Israel, Arafat had sold out the Palestinians. Some even vowed to kill him.

Hamas and the Islamic Jihad

The most dangerous opponents to peace were the radical members of Hamas and a related organization, the Islamic Jihad (jihad means "holy war" in Arabic). Funded in part by the anti-Western Islamic government of Iran, their aim was to establish an Islamic state based on the Koran, the holy book of Islam. Hamas responded to the signing of the peace agreement with bombings and other terrorist attacks on Israeli citizens.

Many of these were suicide attacks. The Islamic religion teaches that anyone who dies fighting a holy war is a martyr who goes immediately to paradise, where he enjoys everlasting bliss. As a result of this belief, many young men who grew up in refugee camps or in the poverty-stricken towns in the occupied territories were willing to become martyrs in suicide bombings. Extremely difficult to stop, the perpetrator of a suicide bombing—

A young Palestinian participates in an Islamic Jihad rally. Groups like Hamas and the Islamic Jihad used terrorism against Israeli citizens to show their disapproval of the peace accord.

most often a young man, sometimes a young woman—strapped dynamite or other explosives to his body. Hiding the explosives under his clothing, he would board a bus in, for example, a major city such as Jerusalem during the busy rush hour, or enter a crowded building such as a shopping mall, and there set off the bomb, killing himself and killing and maiming any unfortunate people who happened to be nearby.

Hamas launched a series of suicide bombings, determined not only to defeat the peace process, but to defeat Arafat and the moderate membership of the PLO as well. On October 19, 1994, a Hamas terrorist bombed a bus that killed at least twenty people. Within a period of less than two weeks in February and March 1996, more than sixty people were killed in four suicide bombings. As of those attacks, nearly two hundred Israelis had been killed by terrorists since the 1993 signing of the peace accord. Following the bombings, however, Hamas lost some of its support from Palestinians who were anxious not to wreck the peace process, and who hoped eventually to establish an independent state. As a Hebron vegetable vendor says, "We are against what is happening in Israel [the bombings]. Everybody in the Palestinian society wants to live in freedom."

Consequences of opposition

Extremist opposition by Jews and by Palestinians has had some far-reaching effects. One of the most important

On February 25, 1996, Hamas terrorists bombed this bus in Jerusalem, killing twenty-two passengers and wounding many others.

An Israeli man grieves for loved ones killed by a Hamas suicide bomber. Terrorism against Israeli citizens has convinced many former supporters of the Palestinian-Israeli accord that peace is impossible.

results of the Hamas terrorist attacks on Israeli citizens was that more and more Israelis turned against the peace accord. Each time an Israeli citizen was killed by Palestinian terrorists, more Israelis became convinced that the peace accord would not work. Arafat and the PLO officials in Gaza and the West Bank could not contain the terrorist attacks, and the promise of "peace for land" was not being fulfilled. Finally, in May 1996 conservative Likud Party leader Benjamin Netanyahu won election as prime minister by the slimmest of margins over Shimon Peres, who had assumed the assassinated Rabin's office, and who

was one of the architects of the peace. Netanyahu's campaign promises included slowing down the peace process and putting the safety and security of Israel first, a message that appealed to many Israelis who feared continued terrorist attacks.

Another important result of the terrorist attacks was Israel's delay in handing over areas of the occupied territories. Israel was afraid that Arafat would not be able to control the violent Palestinian rejectionists, and maintained that an Israeli presence was needed to guard against further terrorism. Palestinians, on the other hand, were angered by Israel's delay in removing its troops from West Bank towns and cities, believing that was a breach of the agreement. Finally, by January 1996, all the agreed-upon territory in the West Bank was turned over to Palestinian rule except the region of Hebron, where large numbers of radical and militant Jewish settlers lived.

Israel's retaliation against the Hamas bombings in early 1996 seemed to derail the peace process completely. Israeli troops set up roadblocks around 465 West Bank communities, confining 1.2 million Palestinians to their hometowns. According to the peace agreement, those towns had been handed over to Palestinian authorities and were autonomous. An angry Arafat complained, "This goes completely against the agreement." The Israelis also sealed the homes of suspected Hamas members and the family homes of the suicide bombers. In Hebron, the Israelis ordered the Islamic University, with 1,500 students, shut down indefinitely.

Border closings

Terrorist attacks also caused Israel to close the Israeli borders between Gaza and the West Bank. Israel feared terrorist suicide bombers from the occupied territories. The temporary closures caused severe problems for Palestinians. Because the economy of the occupied territories was poor, many Palestinians had jobs in Israel. Closing the

Hamas members were partially successful in their efforts to destroy the peace plan. Constant terrorism forced Israel to delay its withdrawal from the occupied territories and to close its borders between Gaza and the West Bank.

borders meant that Palestinians were unable to go to work, which caused them great financial hardship. Following the February/March 1996 bombings, Israel announced it would close the borders "indefinitely."

Extremist Palestinians not only brought fear and death in Israel, they caused turmoil within Gaza and the West Bank, as well. They brought Gaza close to civil war by forcing Arafat's Palestinian Authority (PA) police to use force to stop demonstrations. In November 1994 a battle between Hamas supporters and the PA police resulted in sixteen dead and more than two hundred wounded Palestinians, a death toll comparable to those of the *intifada*, when Israeli soldiers were wielding the guns. The Israelis insisted that Arafat crack down on Hamas and its supporters; at the same time, Arafat could not afford to alienate Hamas sympathizers. Arafat was forced into a delicate balancing act to satisfy both the Israeli demand that he keep the peace and his own need to keep the support of his people.

Israeli guards check a Palestinian family's travel papers at a border checkpoint. Israel closed its borders to the occupied territories to prevent Hamas suicide bombers from entering the state.

The extremist opposition has managed to slow down the peace process and has threatened many times to destroy it altogether. However, many observers believe that Israel and the Palestinians have gone too far to turn back now. The road toward Palestinian statehood and lasting peace between Israel and the Palestinians is sure to have many more difficulties, but to go back would mean returning to more war and bloodshed and destruction, a future no one wants.

Palestinian Authority (PA) police officers wave to crowds as they enter the West Bank. In Gaza, civil war nearly erupted when the PA tried to quell demonstrations by Palestinian extremists.

6

The Road to Independence

REACHING A PEACE agreement was an enormous accomplishment for Israel and the PLO. Establishing an economically stable and prosperous society and a democratic Palestinian state presented greater challenges for the PLO. The most immediate problem the new Palestinian Authority faced was building the economic base of the West Bank and Gaza.

The state of the economy

At the time the peace accord was signed, both Gaza and the West Bank had long suffered from a decayed infrastructure and a poor economy. The PLO had helped maintain much of the social infrastructure in the occupied territories. It funded many necessary social services, helped establish schools, offered scholarships to Palestinian students enrolled at universities elsewhere in the world, and in general helped keep the social infrastructure of the territories functioning. However, the physical infrastructure—roads, power and water lines, school buildings, and hospital buildings—was in need of repair or replacement. Though Israeli companies had helped keep water and power lines operable during the occupation, Palestinian intellectual Edward Said claims that in thirty years "the only thing built [by Israelis] in the occupied territories were prisons."

In addition to the crumbling physical infrastructure, the economic base in the occupied territories was not suffi-

cient to support the inhabitants. Tens of thousands of Palestinians were well-educated and skilled professionals, but many more thousands were unemployed. When the PLO's Palestinian Authority took over the occupied territories, the unemployment rate was about 60 percent. Agriculture was the primary activity in the territories, and in Gaza, on the Mediterranean coast, fishing constituted one-third of the economy. Nevertheless, agriculture, fishing, and the limited small industry were not sufficient for an independent Palestine to prosper.

Palestinian dependence on Israel

Throughout the Israeli occupation, Palestinians were heavily dependent on Israel for employment, for imports, and for export markets. About one-fourth of the population was supported by family members who worked in Israel, usually at low-paying jobs. The territories imported 90 percent of their goods from Israel and exported 70 to 80 percent of their products, mainly agricultural goods, to Israel.

After years of occupation and war, cities in the West Bank suffer from decayed infrastructures and poor economies.

The situation worsened when Israel was subjected to terrorist attacks, both before and after signing the peace accord. Fearful of terrorists filtering in from the occupied territories, Israel tightly sealed its borders. This meant that Palestinian workers could not get to their jobs in Israel, causing severe financial hardships. When Israel closed the borders "indefinitely" in March 1996, unemployment shot up to 70 percent and cost the Palestinian economy millions of dollars daily. Much of the job loss may be permanent because the Israeli Cabinet subsequently voted to allow 16,500 workers from neighboring countries into Israel to take over the construction and farm jobs formerly held by Palestinians. Further, claiming that radicals smuggle fugitives out of and weapons into Gaza by sea, the Israelis blockaded the Mediterranean waters off Gaza, preventing Gaza fishermen from going out to sea.

Building the economy

Nations of the world, especially the United States, were keenly interested in seeing that the peace accord worked. They also knew that any real chance for lasting peace depended on a secure economic base in an autonomous Palestine. However, building an economy is a long, slow process, with problems at every turn.

The task was huge. The cost of rebuilding the physical infrastructure alone was estimated at $3 billion. Immediately following the signing of the peace accord in September 1993, the United States organized a "donors'

Many Israelis and Palestinians wonder if Arafat and his Palestinian Authority will be able to rebuild the battered territories of Gaza and the West Bank. The cost of rebuilding the physical infrastructure of these territories is estimated at $3 billion.

conference" at which foreign governments pledged more than $2 billion over the following five years to rebuild the economy. However, because of continued violence, disorganization, and PLO mismanagement, the money was slow to arrive.

The money was to be spent building housing projects, new sewer systems, roads, and power plants, all of which created some jobs. Another major planned project was a new Mediterranean seaport in Gaza. However, ambitious projects such as these take time, and the many delays caused by terrorist attacks and by Israeli fears of moving too fast pushed back the starting date for many. The World Bank helped finance the seaport project, but as one bank official put it, "It would be amazing if the port were up and running [anytime soon]."

Everyone agreed that either businesses and industries must be developed by Palestinians themselves or Palestinians had to convince foreign companies to come to Gaza and the West Bank. Palestinians needed jobs in their own region, rather than depending upon jobs in Israel. Many Palestinians feared that a stagnant, undeveloped economy would leave masses of Palestinians to become simply a pool of cheap, unskilled labor for Israel.

Some Palestinians took up the challenge quickly. Tahani Abou Daka headed a small clothing factory employing ten people. With the signing of the accord, she planned to enlarge her business and to compete in the Israeli market. As she explained, Arabs in Israel found Israeli products too expensive; Daka planned to meet their need for cheaper products. Yet the economic dependence on Israel was apparent. "Despite the hatred, we are linked economically to Israel," Daka said. "We must continue with them. The important thing is to get money over there and bring it here."

Foreign investment

Most analysts agreed that investment from private companies around the world was essential to boost the Palestinian economy. Many foreign investors considered opening businesses in Gaza and the West Bank. Unfortunately, the continued unrest in the territories, where Hamas and Islamic Jihad members battle Arafat's Palestinian Authority police, frightened private investors, who felt it was too risky to open a business in a region where civil war was a distinct possibility.

Palestinian agriculture was another possible source of prosperity for the country, but that industry, too, faced some problems. Israel is the natural market for Palestinian agricultural products, but Israeli farmers resisted opening the borders to let in Palestinian goods. Palestinians will be forced to develop export markets other than Israel for agricultural and other goods.

Accusations of corruption

One of the biggest obstacles that faced Arafat's PA in building the economy was Arafat's own ineffectiveness as an administrator. Arafat proved himself a wily soldier and an effective politician and self-promoter. However, his administration was accused of inefficiency, waste, and corruption. As a guerrilla fighter, Arafat had received contributions in cash from his supporters in Arab countries, who did not wish to be identified for fear of angering the United States and other Western countries that supported Israel. He was never required to keep formal accounts or report how the money was spent. When he began receiving money from official sources, Arafat had difficulty keeping proper accounts, which slowed up payments for projects in the territories.

Despite his military prowess, Arafat has been criticized as an administrator, and his government has been rocked by rumors of corruption and human rights abuses.

With all of the obstacles to be overcome, Palestinian autonomy did not bring immediate prosperity as many Palestinians had hoped. Many people of the West Bank and Gaza still experienced oppressive poverty, and it may be a long time before their dreams of prosperity and freedom are fully realized.

Supporters of the militant group Hamas parade through the streets of Gaza City. During the occupation, these devoted supporters worked hard to unify the public in resistance to Israeli rule.

Perhaps the greatest challenge the newly independent Palestinians faced was the creation of a democratic administration that truly represented the Palestinian people. Arafat was the uncontested Palestinian leader, but Arafat himself had spent most of the previous decade directing PLO operations from his base in Tunis. He never publicly entered the occupied territories, mainly for fear of capture or assassination by Israeli or Palestinian extremists.

Arafat vs. PLO activists

At the time the peace accord was signed, competing groups of PLO political activists controlled the local politics of the occupied territories. Arafat's Fatah was the most influential group, followed by Hamas and other leftist groups such as the Popular Front for the Liberation of

Palestine. Additional groups organized and oversaw social services in neighborhoods and refugee camps. Political groups dominated by Hamas had maintained contact with Palestinian prisoners in Israeli jails and organized the resistance to Israeli rule during the *intifada*. All these insiders, who had lived the occupation, served the people, and served time in Israeli jails, expected to participate in the new government.

When Yasir Arafat arrived in Gaza on July 1, 1994, to begin the task of establishing Palestinian self-rule, he brought with him members of his Tunisian organization. Many Palestinians viewed Arafat and his organization as outsiders who had just stepped in to take control after the West Bank and Gaza inhabitants had won the battle. Many Palestinians were already critical of the Israeli-PLO agreement and suspected (with good reason) that Arafat would not be willing to include his political opponents in self-rule.

Can Arafat build a democracy?

The most difficult problem Arafat faced in building a truly representative democracy was himself. For forty years, Arafat and the PLO had been used to operating in an atmosphere of secrecy, with Arafat as an authoritarian leader. Those old habits needed to be unlearned for democracy to flourish under Palestinian self-rule, but Arafat did not seem able or willing to take that step. When asked what he thought was the meaning of democracy, he responded, "Democracy is respect for the Palestine National Authority." Arafat seemed to want obedience to his authority more than he wanted to include people with opposing viewpoints.

From the beginning, Arafat showed disdain for his political opponents. He once remarked that anyone who did not like his politics could "go and drink the water of the sea." Arafat was also accused of using repression to silence his opposition by shutting down newspapers that criticized him or his tactics.

Hamas and the Islamic Jihad movements were problems for Arafat from the beginning. They opposed the peace agreement, and they wanted a voice in the new government. Instead of including these voices of opposition in the Palestinian government, as many observers believe he should have done, Arafat used force to try to silence them. Civil war loomed as a real, though unwanted, possibility. According to Ziad Abu-Amr, an expert on Islamic fundamentalism, "All the factions had sworn that they would never resort to violence. Now taboos have been broken. The glass has been shattered."

Strong-arm tactics

The unrest between the PA and opposition groups in the territories and the terrorist attacks on Israeli citizens slowed down the peace process. Under pressure from Israel to stop the attacks, Arafat resorted to strong-arm tactics. Arafat's PA police arrested hundreds of Palestinians. Several of those arrested died in custody, and according to a human rights watch group, many prisoners were tortured or mistreated. Many of the prisoners were arrested not for suspected terrorism against Israelis, but for their political opposition to Arafat's rule.

In February 1995, Arafat set up "state security courts" that admitted sealed, or nonpublic, evidence. The judges were PLO military officers appointed by the PA. Arafat had the final voice on punishments handed down by the courts. He alone could make a penalty harsher or reverse it, as he wished. Many of those tried and sentenced by the courts were members of Arafat's Islamic opposition. To the Palestinians, Arafat's actions were an alarming step toward authoritarian government. However, the U.S. State Department has called them "meaningful measures to crack down on those who plan and carry out terrorism," a statement with which many Israelis agreed. On the other hand, radical Palestinian factions were not willing to bend so easily to Arafat's control. As one Islamic Jihad member warned, "We are the ones who decide when to attack Israeli targets—not Arafat . . . [and] not [the Israeli prime minister]."

In response to the suicide bombings against Israel in February and March 1996, Arafat outlawed the Islamic ex-

tremists. Hundreds of Hamas leaders were arrested in Gaza by the PA. Arafat was praised by Israeli prime minister Shimon Peres, but Benjamin Netanyahu, leader of Israel's Likud Party, accused Arafat of not doing enough to stop the violence and of "sheltering terrorists."

Arafat found himself caught between the Israelis, who wanted him to get rid of the terrorist Islamic groups at any cost, and his own people, who wanted their interests and their political freedom to be the top priority. Many Palestinians argued that it was better to include Hamas in the political process, instead of excluding them, as Arafat had done.

Despite Arafat's hard line, he enjoyed support of the Palestinian people. In January 1996, after Israel pulled its troops from all the West Bank with the exception of the region of Hebron, elections were held for the Palestinian

Palestinian women hold their ballot registration forms and passports while waiting to vote during the first Palestinian general elections.

National Council and for president. Arafat won the presidency with 88 percent of the vote, and Arafat's Fatah won sixty-six of the eighty-eight seats on the council.

With the elections over, the challenge still remained to forge democratic institutions. Many Palestinians feared that the Palestinian National Council would amount to nothing more than a rubber stamp for Arafat, and that he would continue to suppress any voices of opposition. Most observers agree that in order to establish peace in the West Bank and Gaza—and peace in Israel as well—Arafat must give all Palestinians, opponents as well as supporters, a voice in their own government and in their own futures. But whether the newly emerging autonomous regions of Gaza and the West Bank will be shaped by democracy or by authoritarian rule remains to be seen.

7

Jerusalem:
The Holy City

THE THORNIEST OF ALL PROBLEMS facing the Israelis and Palestinians is the status of Jerusalem, a holy place to three world religions: Judaism, Christianity, and Islam.

The city lies at the western edge of the West Bank, the land called Judaea in ancient times, and it is the capital city of the modern State of Israel. The border between Israel and the West Bank runs through the city of Jerusalem, dividing it into West Jerusalem, a modern city with industry, shops, and modern housing, and the older East Jerusalem.

West Jerusalem is the home of Hebrew University, Israel's largest university. Not far from the university campus is the building that houses Israel's parliament, the Knesset. Two ancient holy places are in West Jerusalem: King David's tomb and the place believed to be the site of Jesus Christ's Last Supper. Most of the inhabitants of West Jerusalem are Jews, many of whom arrived after the State of Israel was established in 1948.

East Jerusalem includes nearby villages as well as the Old City, the site of ancient Jerusalem. The Old City is surrounded by forty-foot-high stone walls, most built during the 1500s but some built much earlier. The narrow, cobblestone streets of the Old City are lined with small shops. Here the streets are not wide enough for automobiles, so heavy loads are still carried on donkeys or camels.

The Knesset, which houses Israel's parliament, is located in the modern city of West Jerusalem.

The majority of the residents of East Jerusalem are Arabs. Prior to 1967, East Jerusalem was under the control of Jordan, and Jews were prevented from living in, or even visiting, the city. After the Six-Day War, Israel made the entire city an official part of Israel, and its capital. Unlike the residents of occupied territories, inhabitants of East Jerusalem were given the rights of Israeli citizens. However, little attention was paid to maintaining the utilities and streets of East Jerusalem or meeting the needs of the Palestinian residents. For example, since 1967, 64,880 housing units have been built in the city for occupation by Jewish citizens, while only 8,800 units have been built for Palestinians. According to a study by the Israeli Information Center for Human Rights:

> Since the annexation of East Jerusalem in 1967, the Israeli Government has adopted a policy of systematic and deliberate discrimination against the Palestinian population in all matters relating to expropriation of land, planning and building.

In 1995 the Israeli government earmarked another 140 acres of East Jerusalem to build five thousand housing units, only four hundred of which would be for Arabs. Palestinians saw this as land grabbing and were outraged, and there was such an outcry from the Arab League and from within Prime Minister Rabin's own government that the plan was abandoned.

In 1948 the new nation declared as its capital the coastal city of Tel Aviv-Jaffa because Jerusalem had been designated by the United Nations as an international city. However, following Israel's victory over the Arab forces and its occupation of West Jerusalem in 1948, Israel proclaimed Jerusalem its capital. "Without Jerusalem, we are a body without a soul," said David Ben-Gurion, Israel's first prime minister. But the nations of the world, observing the UN designation, refused to officially recognize Jerusalem as the Israeli capital. To the present day they continue to maintain their embassies in Tel Aviv–Jaffa.

During the 1967 Six-Day War, Israel captured and annexed East Jerusalem, as well; since then, despite the lack of official recognition, Israel has made it clear that it intends to maintain its capital in a united Jerusalem, a city whose history is inseparable from the history of Judaism itself.

Jerusalem is a holy city to Arabs as well, second only to their holiest city, Mecca. In Jerusalem, the prophet Muhammad, founder of Islam, received God's command to spread the message of Islam. Palestinians do not want Jerusalem to be a divided city, but they want to make East Jerusalem the capital of a Palestinian state. Though Jerusalem is not as intimately connected with Islam as it is with Judaism, the Arabs have an eight-hundred-year history in that ancient city.

The holy places

The bitterness with which the Palestinians and the Jews have battled each other for control of Jerusalem comes from the importance of the city to Islam and to Judaism. For the Jews, Jerusalem is their ancient capital and the holiest place on earth. The holiest spot in Jerusalem is the Wailing Wall, or Western Wall. The 160-foot-long wall, which stands on Mount Moriah, is the last remnant of the ancient Temple of the Old Testament. The Temple was destroyed by the Romans in A.D. 70, and the Wailing Wall is all that remains of the western wall of the Temple courtyard. The Wailing Wall takes its name from the many sad cries and prayers said there over the centuries, mourning the Temple's destruction. According to legend, the wall itself still weeps for the destruction of the Temple.

Not far from the Wailing Wall stands the Dome of the Rock, a Muslim holy shrine. With its golden dome, the building is considered the most beautiful building in Jerusalem. Muslims believe that the shrine was built over a rock from which Muhammad rose to heaven accompanied by the angel Gabriel. In heaven, Muslims believe, Muhammad spoke with God, who sent him back to earth to spread the message of a new religion, Islam. According to Jewish belief, on this same rock the ancient Hebrew leader Abraham was ready to sacrifice his son Isaac, as God commanded him to do.

Christians, too, revere several holy places in Jerusalem. The Church of the Holy Sepulcher, built by Emperor Con-

East Jerusalem's Wailing Wall is all that remains of the ancient Temple of the Old Testament. Here, at the holiest site in Jerusalem, worshipers gather to pray before the wall.

stantine in the fourth century A.D., is believed to mark the hill of Calvary, where Jesus Christ was crucified. On Good Friday, the Friday before Easter Sunday, huge crowds of singing and praying Christians follow the route that Jesus took carrying the cross on which he was crucified. The route, known as the Via Dolorosa, or Way of Sorrows, ends at the Church of the Holy Sepulcher.

The Dome of the Rock, one of the Muslim religion's holy shrines, outshines nearby homes and buildings in Jerusalem.

The dilemma of Jerusalem

When the Oslo peace accord was signed in 1993, it was agreed that the status of the city of Jerusalem would be the last issue to be addressed simply because it was so difficult. Peace talks between Israelis and Palestinians over the status of Jerusalem were scheduled to begin in 1996. However, the continued terrorist attacks against Israel delayed the implementation of the peace accord. Exactly when talks about Jerusalem will begin remains uncertain.

A nun prays at the entrance to the Church of the Holy Sepulcher, which Christians consider one of the holiest places in Jerusalem.

A number of possible scenarios for the resolution of the problem have been proposed: two separate municipalities, or cities; one municipality with two separate governing bodies reporting to the municipal government; a joint administration of an undivided Jerusalem by Israeli and Palestinian authorities; international sovereignty, or rule; Israeli sovereignty with some control given to the Palestinian Authority.

Despite Israeli "unification" of the city, Jerusalem is no more unified now than it was before the 1967 war, when Palestinians refused to allow Jews to enter East Jerusalem.

The Palestinians have given up the idea of gaining full control of Jerusalem, but at the same time they refuse to accept the situation as it is, with Israel in control of the entire city. As Faisal Husseini, head of the PLO in Jerusalem, says:

> What good is it to control some area if you cannot go there except with guns, and you cannot enjoy the life there? I think people want to enjoy life in Jerusalem, and not to have all this fighting go on. I accept that the west side of the city is under Israeli sovereignty if the east side is under Palestinian sovereignty. What they cannot say is that all of Jerusalem is under Israel's sovereignty.

Orthodox Jews congregate at the Wailing Wall. Jews, unlike Muslims and Christians, believe Jerusalem is both the worldly and spiritual capital of their people.

While some Jews recognize that they must compromise on many issues to achieve peace, many Jews still feel passionately that the entire city of Jerusalem is theirs by right. Unlike the Arab Muslims and the Christians who see Jerusalem simply as a holy city, the Jews see Jerusalem as both their spiritual and worldly capital.

In September 1995, Israel began a seventeen-month celebration to commemorate the three-thousand-year anniversary of King David's conquest of Jerusalem. In launching the celebration, Prime Minister Yitzhak Rabin declared that the "united Jerusalem is our capital, the capital of the Jewish people, and will remain this way forever."

Palestinians and Israelis have not yet begun to reach an agreement on the status of Jerusalem. However, observers and analysts of the situation do agree on one thing: No one will be completely satisfied with the solution for Jerusalem, but the agreement must be reached or there can be no lasting peace between the Palestinian and Jewish people.

8

Israelis and Arabs in the Middle East: Is Peace Possible?

FROM THE MOMENT of its birth, Israel, a tiny state by any standards, has been surrounded by 160 million Arabs determined to destroy it. When not engaged in outright warfare, Israelis have been the constant target of terrorists. Their homes have been destroyed, their loved ones murdered, sometimes with a cold, deliberate brutality. The smallest Israeli children are routinely taught never to pick up a bag or package that they see lying somewhere—it could contain a bomb. The terrorists have been supported by and taken refuge in Middle Eastern states as diverse as Tunisia, Algeria, Libya, Kuwait, Iran, Iraq, Saudi Arabia, Syria, Egypt, Jordan, and Lebanon.

On the other hand, Israelis have driven Palestinians from their homes, confiscated their lands, and arrested and held them for long periods of time without trial. The dispossessed have lived in miserable poverty in refugee camps in neighboring Arab states, often as unwelcome there as they are in Israel. Palestinians in the occupied territories have been treated as second-class citizens, paying taxes but denied the vote. They have seen their schools closed and been forced to obey strict curfews that sometimes made them virtual prisoners in their own homes. Both Israelis and Palestinians have bitter memories of each other.

A Palestinian woman in Gaza mourns the death of her son and the destruction of her home.

Despite the bitterness, two Arab states, Egypt and Jordan, have made peace with Israel. These two states, who formerly declared that they would push the Israelis into the sea, and who at one time sheltered terrorists and guerrilla fighters, have shown that peace is possible in the Middle East.

The Camp David Accords

In November 1977, just four years after the Yom Kippur War, Egyptian president Anwar Sadat amazed the world by making a trip to Jerusalem to speak before the Israeli Knesset, calling for peace. In September 1978, Sadat and Israeli prime minister Menachem Begin accepted President Jimmy Carter's invitation to engage in peace talks in the United States. While much of the world applauded, Arabs felt betrayed and believed Sadat was selling out the Palestinian cause for American financial aid. The talks were held at Camp David, the presidential retreat in Maryland, and the ensuing two peace agreements, signed in March 1979, were called the Camp David Accords. The first agreement called for Israeli withdrawal from the Sinai, and the second called for Jordan and the Palestinians to join Egypt in talks with Israel about Palestinian self-government in the Israeli-occupied territories of the West Bank and Gaza.

In 1979, Israeli prime minister Menachem Begin (left) and Egyptian president Anwar Sadat (right) engaged in peace talks at Camp David, the U.S. presidential retreat.

Jordan and the Palestinians rejected the offer. Once again the Palestinians passed up a chance for peace and

self-government. The Arab world was outraged that Egypt had broken ranks, and President Sadat paid the ultimate price for his pursuit of peace—he was assassinated in 1981. However, his successor, Hosni Mubarak, continued to honor the peace and managed to reestablish relations with the rest of the Arab world, although Mubarak has also been threatened with assassination.

A Jordanian peace

Jordan fought alongside Egypt and Syria against Israel in the 1967 Six-Day War, in which it lost the West Bank territory to Israel, and again in the 1973 Yom Kippur War. Following the 1967 war, PLO guerrillas set up bases in Jordan, just across the border from the Israeli-occupied West Bank. Huge numbers of dispossessed Palestinians who had fled the Israeli occupation were a source of recruits for the Palestinian guerrillas. However, the fedayeen became so strong that they challenged King Hussein's power, and their attacks on Israel brought Israeli retaliation on Jordan. Finally, in 1970 King Hussein ordered the Jordanian army to drive the PLO out of Jordan.

Even though Jordan refused to harbor PLO guerrillas, other conflicts between Jordan and Israel remained. Disputes over water rights to the Jordan River had been going on since the 1960s when Israel began diverting water from the river for irrigation. Jordan, along with Syria and Lebanon, which also bordered the river, began to divert water from streams that fed into the Jordan River. The water diverted by Jordan was used to irrigate the northern Jordan River Valley.

While the Palestinian-Israeli peace talks were underway, King Hussein prepared to settle the dispute over water rights and to make peace with Israel. A peace treaty was signed between the two countries on October 26, 1994. UN secretary-general Boutros Boutros-Ghali praised the treaty as a sign that peace would continue to spread throughout the Middle East. He expressed the hope that the peace between Jordan and Israel would be followed by full implementation of the Israeli-Palestinian Declaration of Principles, and by new progress in the Israeli-Lebanese and Israeli-Syrian negotiations, leading to a comprehensive, just and lasting peace in the Middle East.

Syria has been one of Israel's most bitter enemies. The two nations had engaged in peace talks on and off, but little progress was made. Syrian president Hafez al-Assad may have felt himself forced to the peace table by the fall of the Soviet Union, his main supporter and source of weapons. The United States was the sole superpower left in the world, and it was Israel's friend. Assad realized that he had few options but peace.

The Golan Heights

The main obstacle to peace between Syria and Israel is the Golan Heights, a two thousand-foot-high plateau of land, 450 miles square, that is strategically important to both Israel and Syria. To the west, the Golan Heights overlooks Galilee, the northernmost part of Israel. To the northeast Golan overlooks Syria; on a clear day the city of Damascus, capital of Syria, can be seen from Golan. Historically, an army that held the high ground of Golan could dominate Galilee and the road to Damascus.

Before Syrian president Hafez al-Assad is able to make peace with Israel, the two nations must come to an agreement about the disputed Golan Heights.

The Israelis captured the Golan Heights from Syria in the 1967 Six-Day War and annexed it, making it an official part of Israel. Israeli soldiers still occupy Golan, infuriating Syria, which stations two hundred thousand troops between the Golan border and Damascus.

Israel has deep reservations about surrendering Golan to Syria. Prior to the 1967 war, Syria deployed gunners who took advantage of the heights to shell Galilean farmers below. Both Israel and Syria realize that for a lasting peace, the Golan Heights must be demilitarized. Both countries

have asked the United States to send troops to guarantee a peace accord, but the U.S. Congress is reluctant to send ground troops to such an unsettled part of the world for an indefinite period of time. Any peace agreement that involves giving up the Golan, even with American troops as a safeguard, would meet with strong opposition in Israel. Israeli prime minister Benjamin Netanyahu has said he will do everything he can to prevent the Golan Heights from being returned to Syria. Furthermore, Jewish settlers living on the Golan Heights are determined that the Golan will remain a part of Israel.

Conflict over water resources between Syria and Israel must also be resolved before a peace agreement can be reached. The Banias River flows across the Golan-Israeli border into the Jordan River, which supplies half of Israel's water. Just before the 1967 war, Syria tried to divert the water of the Banias River away from the Jordan River.

When the Israelis shelled Syrian bulldozers working on the project, Syria shelled farms in Galilee. Israel is unwilling to allow such a situation to develop again. An enduring peace between Syria and Israel must include an agreement to share water.

Lebanon

Lebanon lies on the northern border of Israel. Thousands of Palestinians immigrated to Lebanon in 1948 and the years following. When the PLO was expelled from Jordan in 1970, tens of thousands more Palestinians moved to Lebanon, settling mainly in southern Lebanon, close to the Israeli border. PLO fedayeen launched attacks against Israeli settlements on the border, causing retaliatory attacks by the Israelis. Many believed that the PLO ran a school for terrorists in Lebanon.

The PLO established its headquarters in Beirut and soon was functioning almost like a nation within a nation. It became as unwelcome in Lebanon as it had been in Jordan, but there was little the government could do about it, as PLO strength continued to grow. To make matters worse, civil war erupted in Lebanon between Lebanese Christians and Lebanese Muslims. Arafat tried to keep the PLO out of it, but failed. By the end of the war in 1976, Lebanon was a shattered, ruined country, divided into pockets of hostile factions.

In retaliation for continued PLO attacks against Israel, Israeli troops attacked PLO refugee camps. The PLO retreated to Beirut, which then became a target for the Israelis. Despite Arafat's attempts to control them, radical elements of the PLO continued attacks against Jewish settlements and attacked Jewish civilians elsewhere in the world. Finally, in 1982 the Israelis mounted an all-out attack against the PLO forces in Lebanon that lasted several weeks. The PLO was driven from Lebanon, and the Israelis established a "security zone" in southern Lebanon.

The PLO terrorists were gone, but other, more radical groups moved into Lebanon to take their place. Hezbollah (which means "Party of God" in Arabic), an Islamic fundamentalist group supported by Iran, has been responsible for mounting raids into Israeli territories and shelling Israeli settlements along the border.

The southern Lebanon security zone is an area of about two hundred square miles of Lebanese territory occupied by Israelis to guard against Hezbollah attacks. It is the last region of active fighting between Israelis and Arabs. Despite the attempts at peace talks with Lebanon, in November 1995, thousands of Israelis were forced to take shelter as Hezbollah fighters launched the fiercest rocket attacks against Israel in two years. When Hezbollah fighters continued their attacks, Israel launched a series of attacks on Beirut on April 11, 1996, the first since 1982. The Israelis used helicopter gunships to target offices in Beirut they believed were Hezbollah headquarters. Across Lebanon, Israelis bombed guerrilla strongholds, warehouses where ammunition was stored, and suspected guerrilla bases. Prime Minister Shimon Peres commented that "I hope they learned their lesson, but I can't promise it. If they continue, we will respond." The Hezbollah did continue

In 1982, Israeli troops invaded Lebanon, routing PLO forces and creating a security zone in southern Lebanon.

shelling settlements in northern Israel, and the Israelis continued to respond.

Lebanese officials accused Israel of killing and injuring civilians in violation of peace agreements. However, before Israel attacked Lebanese villages they believed housed Hezbollah guerrillas, they warned villagers to evacuate. As Hezbollah and Israel continued to exchange shelling, more than a hundred thousand Lebanese jammed the highways headed north to escape the hostility. When Israel attacked what Lebanese officials said was an ambulance, killing the occupants, Israel claimed that the vehicle was used by Hezbollah. In another attack, Israel shelled a UN peacekeepers' compound in southern Lebanon, killing more than seventy-five civilians, mostly women and children, and wounding dozens more, in what one UN spokesman called a massacre. Israel claimed that Hezbollah gunners placed just a few hundred yards from the shelter had been shelling Israeli targets, and Israel had retaliated. Hamas and Islamic Jihad terrorists pledged

An Israeli soldier covers his ears as artillery fires at targets across the Israeli-Lebanese border. Soldiers stationed in the security zone defend Israel from Hezbollah guerrillas living in nearby Lebanon.

"Must be something it ate."

more suicide attacks against Israel in retaliation for what they claimed were Israel's attacks against civilians.

A Lebanese government spokesman said that the government did not have the power to dislodge the Hezbollah. However, Syria exercised considerable influence in Lebanon, where it maintained troops to help support the authority of the weak Lebanese government. Israel believed that Syria could have stopped Hezbollah operations if it had wished.

During the attacks of April 1996, Syrian troops helped man antiaircraft guns against Israeli warplanes. The participation of Syrian troops in Lebanon raised fears that war would spread to a full-scale engagement between Syria and Israel. Most observers agreed that as long as the guerrilla attacks continued and Lebanon remained a haven for terrorists, it was unlikely that any peace accord could be reached between Israel and Lebanon or between Israel and Syria.

Iran, Iraq, and the arms race

Iran has vowed to spread Islamic holy war throughout the Arab world, and remains a bitter enemy of Israel and moderate Arab governments, as well as of moderate factions of the PLO headed by Arafat. Iran continues to fund terrorist activities in Gaza and the West Bank, in Lebanon, and throughout the world. Following the suicide bomb attacks in Israel in February and March 1996, Israeli prime minister Shimon Peres issued this statement: "This terrorism is not anonymous. It has a name, it has an address, it has bank accounts. . . . It is spearheaded by a country—Iran. Tehran has become the capital of terror."

Just as threatening to Israel and to Middle East peace is Iraq. As he demonstrated in the 1991 Persian Gulf War, Saddam Hussein of Iraq has expansionist plans in the

Iraq's Saddam Hussein remains a threat to Israel and the hope for peace in the Middle East.

Middle East and continues to call for the annihilation of Israel.

Perhaps the most alarming threat to peace is the arms race that continues in the Middle East, with potentially horrifying consequences. A number of countries have long-range missiles capable of delivering deadly nuclear or chemical warheads at great distances. Iran, Pakistan, and other Islamic states, countries that once seemed far from Jerusalem, are now able to strike Israel directly. Peace agreements are Israel's only defense against these attacks.

The young Palestinian girl in the center is one of the many casualties from the war between Israel and Palestine. Although the war has waged for some fifty years, citizens from both countries long for peace.

The world continues to keep a close eye on Iraq's potential nuclear capability; Iraq has already shown that it will use chemical weapons against its enemies. Israel, Iran, Syria, and Egypt, too, are believed to have developed chemical weapons. The danger of these weapons is that any small-scale engagement can quickly escalate to all-out

war with devastating effects for the Middle East and the whole world. Never before has peace in the Middle East been such an urgent necessity.

Is peace possible?

Ten years ago, many people would not have thought it possible that what was already a forty-year war between Israel and the Arabs over Palestine could be resolved. But Israel and the Palestinians have come a long way: Despite all efforts to destroy the peace process, it continues, although more slowly than many had hoped. The status of Jerusalem is still to be settled. Discussion of Palestinian refugee resettlement is not even on the horizon.

The wider conflict between Israel and other Arab states is even further from resolution. Many Arab states still bear antagonism for Israel and for one another, and there is always the threat that war in the Middle East could erupt as suddenly as a storm in the desert, enveloping Israel, and possibly the world. But as was demonstrated in the dramatic signing of the Palestinian-Israeli accord in September 1993, peace can come just as suddenly. Peace, after all, is what most people in the Middle East want. As one Israeli puts it, "The end of the conflict will mean we can be comfortable in our own skin. We can stop being worriers. We can be Middle Eastern, Mediterranean—we can eat watermelon and sit under our fig trees."

Glossary

anti-Semitism: Hostility toward or prejudice against Jews.

attrition: A gradual wearing down or wearing away; a gradual reduction in numbers.

autonomy: Self-rule.

Dome of the Rock: A beautiful shrine, holy to Muslims, that is built over the spot where Muhammad ascended to heaven to speak with God; it has been called the most beautiful building in Jerusalem.

economy: A system of producing, distributing, and consuming wealth.

Fatah: Literally, "conquest" or "victory" in Arabic; refers to the political and military group founded by Yasir Arafat and others to establish a Palestinian homeland; now the political party of Yasir Arafat.

fedayeen: Literally, "men of sacrifice" in Arabic; refers to Palestinian guerrilla fighters.

Hamas: Literally, "enthusiasm" in Arabic; refers to a group of guerrilla fighters in the West Bank and the Gaza Strip who oppose Israeli occupation.

Hezbollah: Literally, "Party of God" in Arabic; refers to a group of radical guerrilla fighters and terrorists who hope to destroy Israel and set up an Islamic government in Palestine and other Arab countries.

Holocaust: The killing of millions of Jews by the Nazis during the 1930s and 1940s.

infrastructure: The basic equipment and facilities needed by a city or nation to function, such as roads, water and sewer systems, electric and gas lines, schools, and hospitals.

intifada: Literally, "uprising" in Arabic; refers to the uprising of Palestinian people in the occupied territories against Israeli occupation.

Islamic Jihad: A group of radical guerrilla fighters and terrorists who hope to destroy Israel and set up an Islamic government in Palestine and other Arab countries.

jihad: Literally, "holy war" in Arabic; refers to the activities carried out by zealous Muslims to try to establish governments that govern according to the laws of Islam.

Knesset: The Israeli parliament.

Koran: The holy book of the religion of Islam.

Muhammad: The prophet who founded Islam in A.D. 622.

municipality: A town or city with local self-government.

Muslim: Follower of the Islamic religion.

rejectionist: People who oppose, or reject, the Palestinian-Israeli peace accord.

Torah: The written and oral body of Jewish religious law.

Wailing Wall: A holy place to Jews, it is a portion of the western wall of the ruined ancient Jewish Temple in Jerusalem; it takes its name from the cries of sadness of people over the centuries, mourning the destruction of the Temple.

Yom Kippur: A Jewish holy day, the Day of Atonement.

Suggestions for Further Reading

Jonathan Dimbleby, *The Palestinians*. New York: Quartet Books, 1979.

Paul Harper, *The Arab-Israeli Conflict*. New York: Bookwright Press, 1990.

Charles Messenger, *The Middle East*. New York: Franklin Watts, 1987.

Diana Reische, *Arafat and the Palestine Liberation Organization*. New York: Franklin Watts, 1991.

Fawaz Turki, *The Disinherited: Journal of a Palestinian Exile*. New York: Monthly Review Press, 1972.

Richard Worth, *Israel and the Arab States*. New York: Franklin Watts, 1983.

Works Consulted

Lisa Beyer, "Hebron Time Bomb: Settlers Who Provoke," *Time*, March 14, 1994.

———, "The Seeds of Civil War," *Time*, December 5, 1994.

Herbert Buchsbaum, "Enough of Blood and Tears," *Scholastic Update*, September 16, 1994.

Richard Z. Chesnoff, "Facing Up to the Truth," *U.S. News & World Report*, March 14, 1994.

———, "God's City," *U.S. News & World Report*, December 18, 1995.

George J. Church, "No Peace at Home," *Time*, November 20, 1995.

Robert I. Friedman, "Ceding the High Ground," *Harper's Magazine*, April 1995.

Paul Goldberger, "Passions Set in Stone," *New York Times Magazine*, September 10, 1995.

Paul Harper, *The Arab-Israeli Conflict*. New York: Bookwright Press, 1990.

"Israelis Launch First Attacks on Beirut Since '82 Invasion," *St. Louis Post-Dispatch*, April 12, 1996.

"Israeli Troops Blockade West Bank," *St. Louis Post-Dispatch*, March 6, 1996.

"Israel-Jordan Peace Treaty Welcomed," *UN Chronicle*, March 1995.

Baruch Kimmerling and Joel S. Migdal, *Palestinians: The Making of a People*. New York: The Free Press, 1993.

"Letter from Gaza," *New Statesman & Society*, April 28, 1995.

David Lipkin, "Hoping to Reap Profits from Peace," *World Press Review*, November 1993.

"Look over Jordan," *National Review*, August 15, 1994.

David Makovsky and Warren Bass, "On the New Frontier of Peace," *U.S. News & World Report*, September 20, 1993.

Charles Messenger, *The Middle East*. New York: Franklin Watts, 1987.

Muhammad Muslih, "Arafat's Dilemma," *Current History*, January 1995.

Bruce W. Nelan, "All Together Now," *Time*, February 13, 1995.

————, "Raging Against Peace," *Time*, March 14, 1994.

Eyal Press, "Land or Peace," *Nation*, August 22–29, 1994.

William B. Quandt, "After the Israeli-PLO Breakthrough," *Brookings Review*, Winter 1994.

"Rabbis Accused of Promoting Israeli Civil War," *St. Louis Post-Dispatch*, July 14, 1995.

"Rabin's Unrepentant Assassin Gets Life Term," *St. Louis Post-Dispatch*, March 28, 1996.

Diana Reische, *Arafat and the Palestine Liberation Organization*. New York: Franklin Watts, 1991.

Barry Rubin, *The Arab States and the Palestine Conflict*. Syracuse, NY: Syracuse University Press, 1981.

Edward Said, *The Question of Palestine*. New York: Times Books, 1979.

Muhammad al-Sayed Said, "Negotiations That Divide and Conquer," *World Press Review*, November 1993.

"The Second Handshake," *Economist*, May 7, 1994.

Todd Shields and David Makovsky, "Battling over the Holy City of Peace," *U.S. News & World Report*, July 18, 1994.

Fawaz Turki, *The Disinherited: Journal of a Palestinian Exile*. New York: Monthly Review Press, 1972.

Russell Watson, "Peace at Last?" *Newsweek*, September 13, 1993.

Richard Worth, *Israel and the Arab States*. New York: Franklin Watts, 1983.

Index

About the Author

Phyllis Corzine earned a bachelor's degree in literature and language from Webster University and a master's degree in English and American literature from Washington University in St. Louis. She worked as an editor of educational materials for elementary and high school students for five years.

For the past six years, she has taught English and worked as a freelance writer. She has written two previous books for Lucent: *The French Revolution* (1995) and *The Black Death* (1996). Her other work includes a variety of educational materials as well as an adventure novel for young adults.

Corzine, who lives in St. Louis, has three children and two grandchildren. In her spare time she enjoys reading and gardening.

Picture Credits

Cover photo: © Mosha Milner/Sygma
AFP/Corbis-Bettmann, 52, 58, 66, 95
AP/Wide World Photos, 9, 21, 27, 30, 38, 39, 67, 74, 84
Archive Photos, 11, 23, 24, 28, 32, 33, 35
Archive Photos/Consolidated News, 51
Archive Photos/Imapress, 42, 73
© Bill Biggart/Impact Visuals, 65, 71
© Neal Cassidy/Impact Visuals, 70, 85
Corbis-Bettmann, 13
Courtesy: Jimmy Carter Library, 41, 89
© 1990 Thomas Dallal/Impact Visuals, 98
© 1991 Paul Dix/Impact Visuals, 82
© 1992 Dick Doughty/Impact Visuals, 46
© Barry Iverson/Woodfin Camp & Associates, 91
© Tom Krausz/Woodfin Camp & Associates, 80
©Havakuk Levison/Woodfin Camp & Associates, 94
National Archives, 22
Reuters/Bettmann, 49, 97
Reuters/Corbis-Bettmann, 44
Reuters/Rula Halawani/Archive Photos, 63
Reuters/Jim Hollander/Archive Photos, 77
Reuters/David Silverman/Archive Photos, 62
© Henrik Saxgren/2maj/Impact Visuals, 56
© Ellen Shub/Impact Visuals, 47
Sipa Press/Woodfin Camp & Associates, 37, 57, 61
© John Tordai/Impact Visuals, 88
UPI/Bettmann, 16, 19
UPI/Corbis-Bettmann, 83
Yad Tabenkin Archives, 15, 26